# Living on a Boat

An Inexpensive Lifestyle with the Right
Mix of Fun, Adventure, and Relaxation

## Jerry Minchey

# Acknowledgments

I am indebted to my brother, Jim Minchey, his wife Marilyn, and to my son, Brent without their sharing of their vast knowledge and experience of liveaboard boating, this book would not exist.

I am also indebted to my many boating friends who have lived on boats, owned and managed marinas, and especially those who have made their livings by buying and selling boats. I want to thank them for allowing me to pick their brains as I worked on writing this book. They freely shared their knowledge, years of experience, inside information, war stories, and practical tips about living aboard a boat.

Their knowledge and information is what makes this book different from other books about living on a boat. This book is not just my experiences and opinions. The information comes from at least a dozen different experienced liveaboards.

# Contents

# Introduction

*"If you are lucky enough to find a way of life you love,
you have to find the courage to live it."*

~ John Irving

So you want to live on a boat. At least you're thinking about it. It's a wonderful and exciting lifestyle and there are plenty of challenges to keep it interesting.

A lot of people fall in love with the romance of living on a boat without considering the practical part of the lifestyle.

This book is not intended to talk you into living the liveaboard lifestyle. You've probably already talked yourself into that or, at least, into seriously considering the lifestyle.

This book gives you the facts, numbers, inside information, and realistic expectation of living on a boat. And who knows, after reading this book, you may be more convinced than ever that the liveaboard lifestyle is what you really want to experience.

When you learn all of the pros and cons, you might decide that the lifestyle is not as wonderful as you first thought. So let's get started so you can soon find out.

## Is Being a Liveaboard the Ultimate Lifestyle?

Recently, I was talking with several of my friends who have experience living on sailboats, powerboats, houseboats, in RVs, and even one person who lives in a tiny house. In other words, this group of about a dozen people has experience living in every kind of tiny space you could imagine. Well, maybe not. I don't think anybody in the group has lived in a tree house.

We got to talking about the differences between living in an RV and living on a boat, and about the differences between living on different kinds of boats. In addition to talking about the differences between the lifestyles, we also talked about some of the similarities.

We soon brought several other friends who are living on boats, managing marinas, and brokering boats into the discussions.

## Living on a Boat, in an RV or in a Tiny House— Which Is Best?

You are probably wondering why I'm talking about living in an RV or tiny house when this book is supposed to be about living on a boat.

When you're thinking about living on a boat, there's a lot to learn about boats, but there's also a lot to learn about yourself and about living in a small space. That's where input from several different liveaboards, RVers, and from people living in tiny houses can be a big help.

That's one thing that makes this book different. You will be getting information from several people and from people with different small-space living experiences. You'll also learn about the emotional parts of living on a boat and in a small space as well as the practical parts of living on a boat.

There are some good books out there that present the topic of living on a boat mainly from the point of view of one person and I recommend that you read some of them. One of my favorites is *The Essentials of Living Aboard a Boat* by Mark Nicholas.

Whether you're living on a boat, in a tiny houses or in an RV, there's one thing all three have in common. That is, in addition to learning to live in a much smaller space than your three-bedroom house, apartment or condo, you won't have much (almost no) storage space, and you may be leaving your present friends. In other words, there will be a lot of adjusting to do.

For most people this adjusting takes a major change in attitude. Keep this in mind when you're thinking about the liveaboard lifestyle.

When you think about living on a boat, the first thing a lot of people think about is whether they can adjust to living in the small, cramped space. First of all, if you're calling it "cramped," you have two strikes against you already. How about calling it a "cozy" space? You could say that you have a small house, but you have a big yard.

It's all relative. After living in a big house, some people would think living in a one or two-bedroom apartment would be considered cramped.

Meg Seder was one of the contributors to this book. Here is a picture of her tiny house. I'm showing you this photo to help you picture what it would be like if your house was reduced to the size of a boat.

*A 140 square-foot tiny house*

If I showed you a picture of the inside of a boat, it would look a lot bigger than it really is because there wouldn't be much to compare it to. Looking at this picture of a tiny house puts the concept of living in a tiny space more into perspective.

## How This Book Came to Be

The liveaboards in the group were living in a wide range of different boats: small sailboats, larger sailboats (not real large), powerboats, and houseboats. What really helped was that several people had lived in more than one type of boat.

We had many discussions, and, as you might guess, we didn't reach a consensus about which type of liveaboard was better, more relaxing, less expensive or even which lifestyle was more fun.

We did all agree that living on a boat is great way to live—even the members of the group who were presently living in RVs or tiny houses all agreed that the liveaboard lifestyle was the most fun.

I decided to take the questions, comments, war stories, and miscellaneous information from these discussions and add them to my own knowledge and write this book about living full-time on a boat.

I wanted to list all of the contributors as authors, but they insisted that I not do it that way. They said that, since I had written several books, I was the writer. They were the research assistants. Be that as it may, this book wouldn't have existed without their substantial input.

I've relied heavily on them for a lot of the information in this book. I have also relied on them for some of the editing and proofing of this book.

**As I've said before, the unique thing about this book is that it's not based on one person's opinion or experiences.**

**Bottom line:** Over many hours of discussions with a lot of liveaboards, a few beers (well, maybe several beers), and many pages of note taking, revisions, and editing, this book came into being.

In all of our discussions there were a lot of things that we didn't agree on, but the one statement we did all agree on was. . .

*"We had rather be lost at sea than found in a cubicle."*

**Note:** Each chapter in this book more or less stands on its own, so you don't have to read them in order. You can skip around and read the chapters you find most interesting first and then come back and read the other chapters later. Since I've written the book so that each chapter stands alone, if you read this book straight through, you will see some information repeated (because it's relevant to the topic of more than one chapter).

In the *Other Resources* chapter at the end of the book, you will find links to several books, YouTube videos, websites and discussion forums that have a wealth of liveaboard and boating information. After you finish reading this book, start digging into the information in these links, and you will soon be a lot more informed about the liveaboard lifestyle than most people were when they started their adventure.

To sum things up, if your goal is to live on a boat (or to seriously consider the possibility), this book will show you how to make it happen.

# Chapter 1:

---

# Why Do You Want to Live on a Boat?

---

*"As soon as I get on my boat, something inside me changes. Then I really feel what living is."*
~ Laura Dekker

There are many reasons why people choose to live on a boat. Here are some of them:

- Freedom

- Adventure

- Fun

- Inexpensive

- Relaxed lifestyle

- Exciting

- They want a different lifestyle

Why do you want to live on a boat? You might say, "All of the above." But what is your one real reason for wanting to live on a boat? After all, there are other ways that you could enjoy some (maybe all) of the things listed above other than by living on a boat.

You really need to give the question of why you want to live on a boat some serious thought before you jump into this lifestyle. With this question clearly answered it makes the next steps to becoming a liveaboard a lot easier.

Is the liveaboard lifestyle the right choice for you? Maybe and maybe not. That's the purpose of this book— to help you decide if being a liveaboard is right for you.

First of all, living on a boat is not necessarily better or worse than how you're living now, it's just different. It's different in a fun, exciting and adventuresome way. It's a lifestyle many people love, but it's not for everyone.

I'm sure you have a lot of questions, and there are many things you will want to know about the cost, what it would be like on a day-to-day basis, what's involved in this lifestyle, and how you go about making the transition, so let's get started.

## Living on a Boat May Be Ideal for You and It May Not

Making your decision about whether you want to live on a boat (and which type of boat) gets easier the more you nail down why you want to live on a boat. Consider your decision process and your boat selection process as an adventure and enjoy the journey.

Keep in mind that if you do decide that the liveaboard lifestyle is for you, there are a lot of things you will need to learn. There are some great books, websites, and discussion forums out there that will help you continue your education about the liveaboard lifestyle. See the *Other Resources* chapter at the end of the book for my recommendations.

Some people make things happen, some people watch things happen, and some people wonder what happened. I think you'll find that the people you meet at marinas are the ones who make things happen. After all, if they had not made decisions and made things happen, they wouldn't be living aboard a boat. Continue reading and let me show you how you can be one of them.

Knowing why you want to live on a boat is the first step to deciding what type of boat you'll need. Realistically, how are you going to use your boat? A lot of people spend way too much on a cruising "blue water" liveaboard so they can one day sail off into the sunset.

They're not going to do it now, but they want to have that option. Having that option can cost you a lot of money because a cruising boat that is equipped for sailing the open waters is way more expensive than a non-cruising boat.

## There Are Three Broad Categories of Liveaboards

First of all, let me explain that there are two meanings of the term "liveaboard". It's used to describe a boat that someone lives on and it's also used to refer to a person who lives on a boat. It can be a little confusing until you understand the dual meaning of the word.

You could say that you're going to go buy a liveaboard (meaning a boat that you could live on) and then you're going to become a liveaboard (meaning a person who lives on a boat).

In this section when I'm talking about the different categories of liveaboards, I'm talking about the people who are living on the boats, not the actual boats.

**The most common category is the non-cruising liveaboard** who mostly stays in a slip at a marina. This person will occasionally take his boat out for a day or more and even sometimes take the intercoastal waterways to another marina for a weekend getaway.

**The second category is the cruising liveaboard** who is almost always out in the open water and maybe doesn't even have a home port. This is the much less common (but the more romantic) image of a liveaboard. If you want a boat for cruising, you will need one designed for stability and safety, and, of course, you'll need more storage space.

On top of that, you will need a lot of expensive gear such as communication, navigation electronics, and a life raft. You will also want extra parts, tools, and backup systems for everything. For example, extra bilge pumps, a backup radio, and the list goes on and on. In other words, it's not just the cruising boat that's more expensive. You can sink (or should I say invest) a lot of money equipping a boat to be a cruising liveaboard.

How to live the cruising lifestyle is beyond the scope of this book, but I will include some information and comments about cruising as I go along.

**There is a third category of liveaboards who just want to be "floaters".** They're not going anywhere. They just enjoy living on their boat at a marina. This is the least expensive way to enjoy the liveaboard lifestyle. You will find several liveaboards in most marinas who I would call floaters. Many of them don't think of themselves as floaters because they always have plans to be a cruiser sooner or later. They never seem to have everything fixed on their boats. They're never quite ready to sail away. Many of them have not left the marina in years. They're happy. They're living their dream of living on a boat.

**Maybe there is even a fourth category.** Some liveaboards move up and down the east or west coast with the seasons. Even though they are cruising, they are not usually out of sight of land, and they don't need all of the expensive equipment that open water cruisers need.

Keep in mind that your first boat doesn't have to be your final boat or your dream boat. You'll learn later, in chapters 10 and 11, how you can buy your first liveaboard boat, maybe fix it up a little and later sell it for a profit and then get the boat you really want. By that time, you will know what kind of boat you really want.

Some of the liveaboards in our group said that it would be almost impossible for the average person to buy a boat and sell it at a profit. Boats depreciate big time. No doubt about it.

To make a profit on a boat, several things have to happen. First, you have to know the value of the type of boats you're looking for. If you don't know their value, you won't be able to recognize a true bargain when you come across one. You'll also need to know how to negotiate a good deal, and know how to increase the value of a boat by knowing what to fix up and how to do it.

**You make your profit when you buy your boat—not when you sell it.** This is an important point to keep in mind. Very seldom can you sell a boat (or anything else) for more than it's worth, but you can often buy a boat for less than it's worth.

My friends in Jacksonville, FL, bought a 32-foot O'Day sailboat for $10,000, and after doing a lot of work on it themselves, it's worth more than twice what they paid for it now.

Mark said the key to increasing the value of a boat is to spend time and money on the interior. First impressions have a lot to do with the value of a boat. If the inside looks nice, it greatly increases the value of a boat.

Find the Boat That Fits Your Needs for Now

If your dream is to live on your boat at the marina, make short excursions from time to time, and plan to someday cruise the open blue waters, I would suggest that you buy a boat that fits your needs for now and then, someday, when you're ready, sell that boat and get a cruising boat.

A lot of people plan on writing a novel sometime, and a lot of people plan on taking a sailboat and cruising in the Caribbean, but most people never actually do either one. I have a friend who has been "planning" to become a cruising liveaboard for over 20 years and I don't think he has had his boat out of the marina in years.

Spend some time walking around marinas and see how other liveaboards are living and what they're doing day to day. Look at your situation. Are you retired or will you still be going to work every day? Maybe you're not retired and you're still working but you're able to work from your boat. Looking at all of these factors will help you know yourself and know what your needs and wants are when it comes to choosing the right boat for enjoying the liveaboard lifestyle.

**Bottom line:** Be realistic and think about why you want to live on a boat, what you want to do when you're living on a boat, and how you will be using your boat. Think about which of the above categories will you be fitting into now—not what you dream of doing someday.

Be honest with yourself about why you want to live on a boat. When you've completely and truthfully answered this question, you're ready to continue on your journey to becoming a liveaboard.

## Chapter 2:

---

# What Would Life Be Like Living on a Boat?

---

*"A house is but a boat so poorly built and so firmly run aground no one would think to try to refloat it."*

~ Unknown

The first thing you will notice about living on a boat is that you will find that there's a lot more camaraderie when you're living on a boat than you'll find in your present lifestyle.

You may know your neighbors where you live now, but more than likely you don't have much in common with them. You don't share the same interests.

That's not the case with liveaboards. They all share a common interest in boats and the liveaboard lifestyle. Your liveaboard neighbors will likely have a lot of different kinds of boats—sailboats, powerboats, old boats, new boats, large boats, small boats, etc.—but they're all still liveaboards.

## Advantages, Disadvantages, and Other Things to Think about When Considering Living on a Boat

### The Advantages:

- Freedom. You can live where you want to and move with the seasons. You're not tied down. You can change your mind tonight and live somewhere else tomorrow night. You can go wherever whim and chance might take you.

- One of the things many liveaboards like, even more than going to different places, is the freedom to know that they can go if they want to.

- If you don't like your neighbors, you can move to another location.

- You can enjoy international travel and not have to still be paying living expenses back home while you're gone. Just put your boat in storage for a month or so while you're gone.

- Having everything you need handy is one thing liveaboards really like. You will know where all of your tools are, your books, your clothes, etc. Note that many liveaboards who live in a marina have a small storage unit nearby, but it's small enough to still know where everything is.

**The Disadvantages:**

The group had a hard time finding things to list in this section because they all like almost everything about living on a boat. Here are some things that may be considered cons for some people:

- You don't have much privacy in marinas.

- Sometimes there are noises like barking dogs, boats going in and out, etc.

- The constant gentle rocking motion can sometimes be more than just gentle rocking.

- You may not be close to your "back-home" friends. (Of course, they may be reasonably close depending on where you choose to dock your boat.)

**Other Things to Think About:**

- If you are a couple, do you both really want to do it?

- Do you both have hobbies, interests or things you really like to do that don't involve the other person— reading, writing, photography, knitting, crafts, computers, golf, fishing, hiking, painting, jewelry making, etc.?

- If you're not going to have your boat near where you're living now, do you have things or people back "home" that you need to look after or take care of— rental property, aging parents, etc.?

- Headsets or ear buds are mandatory when two people are living on a boat.

- How comfortable are you and your spouse being together 24/7? The little things that annoy you about your spouse can get magnified when you're together 24/7 in a small space. Most people need a little time apart. There are ways to do this while living on a boat, but give it some consideration. Be sure to schedule some "me" time. Of course, if one or both of you are working away from the boat that will give you some time apart.

- Just like in a stick-and-brick home, there will be unexpected maintenance expenses from time to time. Allow for these expenses in your budget.

- If you act like a tourist and want to eat out a lot and see and do things like a tourist, you will end up spending money like a tourist. To keep your expenses low, you have to remember that you're not on vacation.

- Life on a boat can be much less expensive than living a traditional stick-and-brick lifestyle—but you have to learn a few secrets and techniques covered in later chapters.

Liveaboards are a diverse bunch. There are doctors, lawyers, school teachers, airline pilots, and Indian chiefs living the liveaboard lifestyle. (Well, I haven't actually met any Indian chiefs.)

Even though I talk about spouses and couples in this book, you will see a lot of solo liveaboards. There are several websites where solo liveaboards share their concerns, fears, stories, etc. I talk a lot more about living solo on a boat in chapter 19.

## More on What It's Like to Live the Liveaboard Lifestyle

The cost of living on a boat can be substantially less than living the traditional lifestyle in a house or apartment.

One woman in the group said, "When living the liveaboard lifestyle, you will also save a lot of money by not buying things you don't need. **Going shopping will no longer be considered a form of entertainment.** There's no place to put things you don't really need." How many pairs of shoes do you need? "

Another member of the group said, "I had not thought about it, but she's right. I don't buy 'stuff' like I used to. I did buy a new pair of shoes the other day, but I also threw out an old pair. There's no room to accumulate things."

One good way to learn more about what it would be like living the liveaboard lifestyle is to talk to people who are doing it. If you don't know anyone personally, the next best thing is to watch some interviews with people who are living on their boats. Listen as they talk about their experiences.

## Below Are Some Links to YouTube Videos Showing the Cruising Liveaboard Lifestyle:

https://www.youtube.com/watch?v=CkaH_UUH0Ek

https://www.youtube.com/watch?v=sF9TNM9R-iw

## Here Are Some Links to YouTube Videos Showing Liveaboards Living at a Marina:

https://www.youtube.com/watch?v=g8Rbt1u2Ljs

https://www.youtube.com/watch?v=KKkNKEJ_Pfg

These four videos are not necessarily the best or most popular, just representative of the types of videos you can find on YouTube about living on a boat.

Of course, when you get to these videos, you can keep clicking and watch as many videos about liveaboards as you have time for. I would suggest that you watch a video or two every few days. It's a great way to learn about the lifestyle. Keep in mind that most of the videos show the glamor and the good parts—not the storms, ripped sails, and engines that won't crank.

Since you can't watch all of the liveaboard videos, I would suggest that you select the ones with the most views. They are usually the best and most informative ones. Who knows, one day you may be posting your own liveaboard videos.

## What Would You Miss about Your Old Lifestyle?

A lot of non-boaters ask liveaboards this question, but the group couldn't think of much they would miss about their previous lifestyle. They said that it would be easier to list things they would miss if they gave up their liveaboard lifestyles. Here are some of the things they agreed they would miss if they gave up living on a boat:

- Hour-long coffee times with friends

- Spending time with wonderful, like-minded friends

- Sunrises and sunsets over water

- Never having to deal with snow and cold weather

- Always having friends nearby to have a glass of wine with from time to time without having to take more than a few steps

- Sitting around talking with interesting friends

- In other words, total freedom

One thing that most of the liveaboards in our group agreed on was that their biggest regret was that they didn't embark on this lifestyle sooner.

## Make Your Decision

The information in this book, along with the links, references and other books I recommend, will give you the information you need to make your decision—but you have to make the decision.

I remember being in a marketing class at Harvard one time and the professor asked a student what he would do in a case being studied. The student said he would go out and get more information. That was the wrong answer.

The professor said, "Every decision you make for the rest of your life will be made with incomplete information. Do a reasonable amount of research and investigation and then make a decision. If it's wrong, you can change it." He added that businesses lose more money by not making a decision than they ever lose by making a wrong decision.

I think that concept applies to personal decisions too.

## What If You Change Your Mind about Being a Liveaboard?

The liveaboard lifestyle is not for everyone. Not everyone is cut out for this lifestyle, individually or as a couple.

Selling your boat can be done easily in a matter of weeks unless you're trying to get the absolute top dollar for it. In fact, you can list your boat on eBay and sell it even quicker.

The boat broker and marina manager in our group both said that most boats don't sell this fast, but they agreed that many people think their boats are worth a lot more than they're really worth. They did say that when boat owners finally get around to setting a realistic price and are willing to negotiate a little, they can usually sell their boats fairly quickly.

You are not locked in. You can change your lifestyle in a heartbeat. And if you do your homework and find a great deal (and do a good job of negotiating) when you buy your boat, you can possibly sell it for more than you paid for it.

**Bottom line:** Do a reasonable amount of research, soul-searching and fact-finding and then make your decision. You will never have all of the information, but remember when you're living the liveaboard lifestyle, it's easy to change your mind, sell your boat and live a different lifestyle. Keep reading and then make your decision.

# Chapter 3

# How Much Will It Cost to Live on a Boat?

*"A rising tide doesn't raise people who don't have a boat."*

~ Rahul Gandhi

Living on a boat can be a very inexpensive lifestyle, but it can also cost a fortune. It's your choice. Well, maybe it's not always your choice. You may start out with an inexpensive boat and then one thing after another breaks, squeaks, leaks or comes loose. On top of all of that, you keep finding neat gadgets that you want to have on your boat. The first thing you know you've spent a lot of money.

If you can do a lot of the maintenance yourself (and you don't keep buying gadgets for your boat), being a liveaboard can be a very inexpensive lifestyle.

**The philosophy of a true boater:** "You should not have kids until you can afford them. When you can afford kids, you should buy a boat. Later, when you can afford kids and a boat, then you should buy a bigger boat. There's no limit to how big of a boat you can buy."

## An Overview and Description of Boating Expenses

The following example is for a 30-foot sailboat that was bought for $25,000 and is being kept docked at a marina and not used for much cruising. Larger or more expensive boats would cost proportionally more. And, of course, if you have a cruising boat, you can expect your expenses to be more for maintenance, but you won't have the liveaboard fees or the slip fees, although there will be some docking fees.

Maintenance: $100 to $200 a month. Compared to your present house or apartment, you will find that things on a boat break more often. Boats are constantly being rocked by the waves (or should I say being thrashed around by the waves). On top of the constant battering your boat is subject to (even if it never leaves the marina), water deteriorates everything and salt water is ten times worse. Even if you're on a calm, freshwater lake, your boat is still going to need a lot of maintenance. It's the nature of the beast.

How much will all of this maintenance cost you? The numbers can run all over the charts. It depends on how big, how complicated, how much equipment, the condition, how old your boat is, and, of course, how much of this work you can (or will) do yourself. A lot of people enjoy working on their boats, and if you do, there are almost an unlimited number of projects you can undertake. The longer you live on your boat the more you'll learn about how to fix things.

I know you would like for me to put a dollar figure on all of this. There are a lot of variables, but if you have to have a number, I would say go with 5% to 10% a year of the value of your boat. That's right; for example, if you spent $25,000 to buy your boat, plan on $1,250 to $2,500 a year to maintain it. That would be roughly $100 to $200 a month. And that's based on you doing a lot of the basic maintenance yourself.

If you have a boat that's in good condition to start with, and you do a lot of the maintenance yourself, you might get by on the low end of these numbers.

Keep in mind that a lot of people don't spend much on maintenance and just let their boats deteriorate and lose value. My recommendation is to do the opposite and not only do the necessary maintenance but constantly be improving your boat. Many of the liveaboards I know tell me that their boat is worth more now than they paid for it. That takes a lot of improvement because boats generally depreciate just like a car.

If you don't enjoy working on a boat, are you sure you want to be a liveaboard?

Insurance: $100 to $150 a month.

Utilities: $50 to $150 a month depending on whether you have an air conditioner and your usage. This is for water, electricity and sewer and gray water pump-out, and maybe WiFi. It doesn't include your cell phone.

Slip Fees: $250 to $400 a month.

Storage: $50 to $100 a month depending on how big of a storage unit you need.

Liveaboard Fees: $50 to $100 a month. This could vary a lot depending on what is included.

Miscellaneous Expenses: $200 to $500 a month. There are a lot of miscellaneous expenses that you could have from time to time. Sometimes these expenses are included in some of the above listings and other times not. This includes things like parking at the marina, a diver to change the zincs and scrub the hull, painting the bottom, annual taxes and registration.

## Summary of the Monthly Costs to Live on a Boat:

Note that personal expenses such as food, clothing, cell phone, medical expenses, medical insurance, and owning and maintaining a car are not included.

The expenses shown below are based on living on a small $25,000, 30' sailboat. There is no upper limit on the price of a boat or the expense of living on one, but you can enjoy the liveaboard lifestyle on less than the amount shown below.

A lot of the costs are proportional to the size and price of your boat, but, of course, not all of them are. Your cell phone, internet, parking, and storage won't go up or down with the cost or size of your boat but most everything else will, so you can use the numbers below to get a rough idea of how much it will cost you to live on a boat and you can see if the numbers fit your budget.

The good news is that you may find that living on a boat is less expensive than the lifestyle you're living now.

**The total of the expenses listed above is $800 to $1,600 a month.** This is assuming that you are not making payments on your boat. As you can see, that's a wide range and the best I can say about the monthly cost is that it depends. And as I said before, this number does not include food and personal expenses.

The three main variables are how much maintenance you can do yourself, how many creature comforts you want, and how nice of a marina you want to stay in.

Keep in mind that the above expenses are for living in a marina (which is the most common liveaboard lifestyle). If you live on the hook, your expenses would be less. If you spend most of your time cruising, your monthly expenses could be a lot less. Keep in mind that the initial cost of getting your boat equipped and ready to cruise would be a lot more and also the cost to maintain the extra equipment would be more.

## Three Points to Keep in Mind:

1. Don't push the limit of your budget when you buy your boat. There will always be expenses when you buy a boat regardless of how good a condition it seems to be in.

2. Always keep a reserve fund available. This is particularly important when you're cruising.

Expensive maintenance problems can pop up at the most inconvenient times and there will always be unexpected expenses when you own a boat.

3. Learn as much as you can about your boat and do as much of the maintenance as you can yourself. This cuts the cost of being a liveaboard considerably and it builds your confidence. The ability to fix most things on your boat is especially important when you're cruising.

**Bottom line:** As you can see, it's possible to live the liveaboard lifestyle for much less than living in a conventional stick-and-brick home. But on the other hand, living on a boat can get very expensive if you let it.

# Chapter 4

# Liveaboard Life—Pros, Cons, and Things to Consider

*"One of the most tragic things I know about human nature is that all of us tend to put off living. We are all dreaming of some magical rose garden over the horizon instead of enjoying the roses that are blooming outside our windows today."*

~ Dale Carnegie

Living on a boat is a different kind of life. It's not necessarily better or worse. It's just different. Being a liveaboard is not the best lifestyle choice for most people. Even though a lot of people dream of living the carefree, liveaboard lifestyle, many of them wouldn't be happy—at least, not for very long.

That's not all bad. If everyone (or even a lot of people) really did choose to live on a boat, it would be chaos at the marinas. I like the status quo. The good news is that there's room at the marinas for one more boat—yours.

While many people are dreaming of living the liveaboard lifestyle, you're doing more than dreaming. You're taking action (you bought this book), and you're getting the facts to see if this is the right lifestyle for you. Here are some of the facts that you need to know and consider.

## Pros

- It's a romantic life (at least everyone thinks it is).

- It's an inexpensive way to live (at least it can be).

- The gentle rocking makes for great sleeping (until the rocking becomes much more than gentle).

- You get to enjoy sunsets or sunrises or maybe both.

- You get to smell the salt air (if you're on the ocean).

- You can take off and go cruising at the drop of a hat.

- There are fantastic views at night.

- You're free to move your "home" any time the mood hits you.

- The two things most people enjoy the most are the freedom and the lifestyle.

- You'll enjoy a lot of camaraderie, and your life won't be boring.

- You have the ability to leave civilization on a whim (at least for short periods of time).

- It's an interesting, exciting, and different life.

## Cons

- It's not as romantic as books, movies, and TV make it out to be.

- The gentle rocking can get to be much more than just gentle.

- Boats can be (and usually are) damp, particularly in the winter.

- Fighting mold can be a constant challenge.

- One concern is storage—there ain't none.

- The toilet—it's cramped, uncomfortable and it smells.

- You literally take all of your crap with you everywhere you go.

- There is always something on a boat that needs fixing.

- Not having your own washer and dryer.

- Each day you get to decide whether to fix something that's broken or do preventive maintenance.

- If you're in a marina, you're very close to your neighbors and you know what they're having for dinner.

- Unexpected expenses can seemingly drop out of the sky.

## Things to Consider

The liveaboard lifestyle takes some getting used to and some changes in the way you think.

Some of these changes won't come about immediately. Your thoughts and feelings will change over time. The first thing that most liveaboards have to adjust to is that the cabin space seems ridiculously small. They knew this going in, but it doesn't really sink in until they actually start living on the boat. They accept the fact and decide that they can put up with the small space to get to enjoy the liveaboard lifestyle.

After some time they don't look at it that way at all. Most tell me that they feel like they have all the space they need. They say they don't even want any more space. They like their small space.

One liveaboard stated it this way. He said, "I realized recently that one of the things I like about living on my boat is that I don't have to hunt for anything. Every single item has a place, and it stays in its place. If an item doesn't have a place then it doesn't need to be on the boat, and I get rid of it (or put it in my storage unit). If I want something to be on my boat, and I don't have a place for it, I get rid of something I'm not using and make a place for the new item."

I think that describes how a lot of liveaboards feel.

Here's another comment that describes how liveaboards feel after they adjust to living on a boat. One member of our group said, "I was visiting a friend recently who lives in a traditional house. I wanted to go to the bathroom, and I had to walk way down the hall twice as far as the whole length of my boat. I remember thinking, *This sure is a long way to have to go to get to the bathroom.*

**Bottom line:** When you live on a boat, over time you start thinking about space and stuff in a whole different way. You will soon realize that you don't need much of either. There are a lot of pros and cons, but the pros will outweigh the cons (if they didn't, you wouldn't continue to be a liveaboard). Expect that it will take some time for you to adjust to the liveaboard lifestyle. You will start enjoying your new lifestyle immediately, but it will take time before it becomes natural. Enjoy the transition.

# Chapter 5:

## Sailboat, Powerboat or Houseboat?

*"In certain places, at certain hours, gazing at the sea is dangerous. It is what looking at a woman sometimes is."*

~Victor Hugo

Deciding whether you want a sailboat or a powerboat is like trying to decide if you want a dog or a cat. And, of course, a houseboat is a different animal altogether.

There may be a few people who honestly don't yet know which type of boat they want. As one boat salesman told me, "If you don't know which type of boat you want yet, you're nowhere near ready to buy a boat."

Even after you know which type of boat you want, there are several things to consider before you make your final selection. Things like old vs. new, fiberglass vs. wood, small vs. large, and then there's price range, amenities, etc.

My guess is that you probably already decided which general type of boat (sailboat, powerboat or houseboat) you want even before you bought this book. Nothing I'm going to say is going to change your mind.

## What If You Have No Idea Which Type of Boat You Want?

Just in case you don't know which type of boat you want, I'll go over some basic differences and some pros and cons of each type.

There is a lot of logic that could go into the decision, but there is also a lot of emotion. When you finally make your decision and someone asks you why you made that choice, the only true answer may be, "I just decided that's the boat I wanted."

There is a lot of emotion and gut feel that goes into selecting the type of boat you want. But let's factor some logic into the decision process. Consider the pros and cons of sailboats versus powerboats and that may help you decide.

This chapter is mainly about deciding between a sailboat and a powerboat. After all, a houseboat is a version of a powerboat. My son lived on a houseboat for a several years on one of the TVA lakes. He lived on the hook in one of the many coves. He had to move to a different cove every two weeks to be in compliance with the TVA rules.

## Should You Consider a Houseboat?

There is a lot of room on a houseboat, and it's an inexpensive way to live, but it's not nearly as much fun as living on a sailboat. You can get some real bargains on houseboats, and that's one of the options you should consider if you want to be a liveaboard and you're on a tight budget.

If you're considering a houseboat, the two basic types are pontoon boats and monohull boats. A pontoon boat is faster and more fuel efficient, but it rocks like mad with the smallest wave. My son lived on a 40-foot monohull. He never lived on a pontoon boat.

From what I've heard friends say, most of them would not go with a pontoon boat for a liveaboard even though some of my friends who live on pontoon boats love them.

## Sailboats vs. Powerboats

- A sailboat is stabler both at the dock and on the open water than a powerboat. This is because of the lower center of gravity. In other words, a sailboat won't rock as much and you can sleep better. You can also handle bigger waves in a sailboat than you can in a powerboat.

- Sailboats are slow. It can take forever to get to your destination.

- A powerboat can burn through fuel at an alarming rate. You can spend several hundred dollars on fuel just for a short weekend outing.

- A sailboat is generally less expensive to maintain, even though sails and rigging repair or replacement can get expensive.

- Powerboats have more storage.

- My son said, "I've owned both sailboats and powerboats. I like sailboats better, and that's what I presently have."

- My brother, who has lived on powerboats and sailboats, told me that the one thing he disliked the most about a sailboat is that you can't be on a tight schedule. He told me that when he went out for a weekend outing and had to be back to work on

Monday morning, he couldn't wait until late Sunday afternoon and then head back to the marina when he had a sailboat. If he did, and the wind died down, he might not make it back in time.

- With a powerboat, you can push a button and be out to sea in a matter of minutes and get there in short order. It takes longer to get a sailboat going and then it takes a lot longer to get anywhere.

- Fuel costs and engine maintenance for a sailboat are almost non-existent.

- Powerboats have larger and more comfortable living areas and usually more headroom. You can generally stand up in all parts of a powerboat but not in many sailboats.

- A center-cockpit sailboat generally will have larger living quarters than an aft-cockpit sailboat, but there are other tradeoffs, so look at a lot of sailboats to get a feel for which boat is best for you and your needs.

- With a sailboat you can trade-off performance for comfort and living space in a given size boat. If you're going to be mainly staying at the marina, the comfort and living space are probably more important, but to get this you will have to give up being able to sail when there's not much wind.

- One of the biggest trade-offs with a powerboat is performance and fuel efficiency. There is a broad range of miles per gallon in powerboats. Be sure you know what the true fuel consumption numbers are for the boat you're considering and compare that to how you plan to use the boat.

- Wind is cheap (and slow). Fuel is expensive (and fast).

At this point, your goal should not be to buy your dream boat. You goal should be to buy a boat that you can sell at a profit when you have enough experience to know what kind of boat really is your dream boat. Chapters 9, 10, and 11 go into details about how to buy your boat and get a really good deal.

**Bottom line:** As I said at the beginning of the chapter, your mind was probably already made up about whether you wanted a sailboat or a powerboat before you read this chapter and nothing I've said has likely changed it.

Take a serious and realistic look at how you plan to use your boat and get the one that gives you the most joy. After all, that's one of the biggest reasons to live on a boat.

# Chapter 6:

---

# Cruising vs. Living at a Marina

---

*"Any damn fool can circumnavigate the world sober. It takes a really good sailor to do it drunk."*
~ Sir Francis Chichester
as he was loading his boat with gin

Cruising on the open blue water in the Caribbean or cruising around the world is what comes to mind for most people when they think of living on a boat. And that's the dream and eventual goal of a lot of liveaboards when they're first thinking about becoming a liveaboard.

By the way, the USA's 2010 Naval Operations Concept defines blue water as "the open ocean," green water as "coastal waters, ports and harbors," and brown water as "navigable rivers and their estuaries."

The reality is that most liveaboards never cruise the open ocean. They may go out to sea for a few days or take the inland waterways to get to a different marina, but they don't live off the hook or sail the Caribbean. They have a home base at a marina.

Most liveaboards have found that living on their boat at a marina gives them the inexpensive lifestyle they were looking for with the right mix of fun, adventure, relaxation, and camaraderie they want.

## What about Cruising?

By all means, cruising should not be undertaken by anyone who doesn't have extensive boating experience. It's ok to have the idea in the back of your mind for "someday".

You can't learn to cruise by reading a book any more than you can learn to play a musical instrument or learn to play golf by reading a book. Don't get me wrong. You can learn a lot by reading books, watching videos, and reading posts on discussion forums, but to really learn what you need to know to be even somewhat prepared for cruising you need to take some lessons, and, if possible, spend some time as a crew member actually cruising with an experienced captain.

The purpose of this chapter is not to talk you out of cruising and by no means is it intended to teach you what you need to know to become a cruiser.

The purpose of this chapter is to give you some information about cruising, point out some of the things that are very different from the normal liveaboard lifestyle, and help you decide if one day you really do want to cruise the open waters. Let's get started.

When you're a liveaboard at a marina, your main goal is comfort, but your main goal as a cruiser is safety. When you're cruising, your boat, the equipment, and your crew must all be prepared.

Cruising can be less expensive than paying rent at a marina, but getting your boat and equipment set up and ready for cruising will be expensive—maybe even very expensive. Not only will you need a lot of extra equipment, but you will need backups for almost everything. For the important things like a bilge pump it would be a good idea to have a backup for your backup. You will need extra sails and a lot of tools for making repairs. You'll also need backups for your communication and navigation equipment. And, of course, by all means, you will need a fully stocked ditch bag (which I'll describe later).

After you've done a lot of studying and reading about cruising, the next thing you need to do is take lessons or sign on to be a crew member on a few trips with knowledgeable and experienced captains. You need to spend time in some rough weather. After a few days in some heavy seas (and maybe getting seasick), you may decide that cruising is not what you want to do after all.

If this turns out to be the case, learning this before you spend a lot of money on equipment and possibly money on a more expensive boat than you would need to be a liveaboard at a marina, you could find out that being a crew member on a cruising adventure was a valuable learning experience.

Of course, if you do decide that cruising is what you want to do, start learning everything you can about your boat (its engine, equipment, and systems). Begin acquiring the tools you will need to repair almost everything on your boat. You need to know your vessel inside and out.

One advantage of having all of this knowledge and being able to repair almost everything on your boat is that you will save a lot of money by doing most of your own maintenance.

My brother told me about a course he took at the local technical college in how to repair small diesel boat engines. On the final exam, each student had an engine in the shop that had several things wrong with it. The instructor said that this exam was just like when you're sitting out in the ocean with a dead engine—when you can get it to crank, you can go home.

He said that he finally got his engine to crank and run. He said that in a real situation there probably wouldn't have been so many things wrong with an engine all at one time. On the other hand, if the boat was rocking (maybe even rocking big time), and it was hot (or cold), and you were working in cramped quarters like you would be when you were stranded at sea with a dead engine, fixing the engine would be a lot harder than doing it in the air conditioned shop with the engine bolted to a workbench where it was easy to get to everything.

## Murphy Was a Cruiser

To be a cruiser you have to be prepared to overcome everything Mother Nature, other boaters, and Murphy's Law can throw at you. In fact, I think Murphy was a cruiser because if it can go wrong, break, or malfunction while you're cruising, it will. You have to be prepared to fix it, replace it or make adjustments and live without it.

There's also the possibility of being approached by pirates. You could be armed, but they could be armed better. From past news accounts, it looks like a shotgun might be the best weapon to have on board. But be careful going into (or even near) other countries. Take a gun into a Mexican dock and you could be in big trouble.

In many cases, your life and the lives of your crew, family, and guests will literally depend on your knowledge, skills, and the speed with which you can make decisions and take actions to take care of situations. By the way, when I say, "situations," maybe that's a politically correct way of saying, "problems."

## Cruising vs. Living at a Marina—Maybe You Can Do Both

Here is how my son described one of his cruising adventures: "Even though I mainly live at a marina or live on the hook, I do enjoy cruising from time to time. Some of the most fun I've had cruising has been when I was able to take some interesting cruising trips as a crew member on other people's boats.

"The most fun and exciting cruise I can remember was when two friends and I were able to sail as part of the crew of the tall ship the A. J. Meerwald from NJ to Boston. The A. J. Meerwald is the state of New Jersey's officially designated tall ship. It's a restored 1928, 115-foot, Oyster Schooner.

"Below is a picture of the ship and a picture of me with my two friends, Bill Stegal, and Robert Loest. (I'm the one in the middle.) As you can tell from the picture, we were one happy crew."

One of the advantages of living in a marina is that quite often neighboring liveaboards will be getting ready to go cruising and will be looking for another crew member or two to go along on the trip. If your schedule is flexible, you'll likely find some great opportunities.

In addition to having fun, sailing with other sailors who are experienced at cruising is a great way to learn and become a more knowledgeable and confident cruiser.

You can learn a lot this way and not have to pay for as many sailing lessons.

Note that I talk some more about cruising in chapter 19 when I talk about living aboard solo.

**Bottom line:** Keep your dream alive about one day becoming a cruiser. Learn how to fix everything on your boat, and sign-on as a crew member with an experienced cruising captain when you have the opportunity. Gaining all of this knowledge and learning the skills needed to be a cruiser is fun and exciting. Later, if you decide that you're ready to be a cruiser and that it's the lifestyle you want to live, you will be prepared to take on the challenge. And even if you never become a cruiser, you'll have a lot of fun along the way learning how to be one.

## Chapter 7:

---

# Living on the Hook—the Art of Floating for Free

---

*"The tragedy of life is not that it ends so soon, but that we wait so long to begin it."*

~ W.M. Lewis

In the phrase, "On the hook," the hook that's being referred to is the anchor (it looks like a hook). So when you're living on the hook you're living tied to an anchor. And if you're tied to an anchor, you're not tied to a dock at a marina.

The best part about living on the hook is that it's free. You're not paying a monthly fee to a marina.

While we're talking about living on the hook, there's another popular boating phrase, "Living off the hook." That phrase means that you're cruising the open water and not tied to an anchor.

One member of our "Boat-Book Roundtable" said, "I've lived on the hook for a year or so at a time on TVA lakes. I would take my dinghy and come into the dock where my car was parked from time to time. Then I would go into town for supplies and to socialize with friends."

He also said, "I've lived at a marina on the coast of Florida too (in a sailboat boat). In a nutshell, living at a marina is more fun but more expensive. Take your pick."

## Living on the Hook Is Nice, But. . .

Living on the hook is not as wonderful as it first sounds. Yes, not paying a monthly fee to a marina sounds like a great idea, and in some cases it can be. If your goal is to get away from it all and have uninterrupted time to write the great American novel, or you want to finish your thesis, it might be the perfect solution. Living on the hook is also nice if you sometimes want to be like

Winnie the Pooh when he said, "Sometimes I sits and thinks and sometimes I just sits."

But there are downsides. Whether you're on a lake, out in the ocean or up a river, there will be rules that you will have to follow. A lot of places will require that you move every two weeks. And, of course, you can't dump black water or even gray water, so you will have to come into the marina every couple of weeks.

That's not all bad. You will need to get supplies and maybe you will need at least a little bit of socializing time.

By the way, in regards to taking a bath, you could just take a bar of soap and jump overboard—that's what one member of our group said he did for a couple of years. He said that sometimes the water got very cold and even a quick bath was brutal. Even when he was out in a secluded cove, he said that he still wore a swimsuit. He learned that boats could come by faster than he could scramble and get back on his boat. Jumping overboard to take a bath saves fresh water and allows you to go longer without having to empty your gray water tanks, but, as was said, it can be brutal in cold weather.

One disadvantage to keep in mind when you're considering living on the hook is that most of the places where you drop your anchor will be more exposed to waves and wind than when you're at a marina, so you can expect a lot more rocking—maybe even too much in bad weather.

Two more things to consider when you're living on the hook are, when you take your boat or your dinghy to the dock, where are you going to park it, and where are you going to leave your car parked while you're out on the hook?

Some city or county owned marinas will allow boats to come in and pump out their tanks and fill up with fresh water free of charge and others charge for this service.

If you're just coming in occasionally for supplies and to socialize, you can usually pick a time when the weather is good, but if you're coming in every day to go to work, you could arrive at work wet or sweaty.

Something else to think about is how secure your dinghy will be when you tie it up at the dock. If you have a motor on your dinghy instead of relying on oars, that could make your dinghy even more of a target for theft.

Keep in mind that some areas where boats anchor are a haven for riff-raff and people using drugs. Be sure to check out any area where you're considering anchoring.

Just like on land, there are good neighborhoods and bad ones.

I highly recommend that you spend at least three months living at a marina before you decide to start living full time on the hook. This way you can get used to living on your boat and make sure you can adjust to the lifestyle and small quarters. Also, while you're living at the marina, you can make short excursions and live on the hook for a few days at a time while you still have your dock to come back to.

## Some of the Downsides of Living on the Hook

Probably the biggest hassle is that everything you use has to be hauled to your boat. You have to haul food, jugs of water, ice, and other supplies. You won't have air conditioning or refrigeration. At times, when you have to get in your dinghy and go ashore when it's raining and there are three-foot waves because you're out of water or toilet paper, or some other necessary supplies, you realize that living on the hook is free, but it's a rough way to live.

Another thing to consider is that there's not much security when you're living on the hook or tied to a mooring ball. Maybe, if there are other boats around, there is a little security, but not much. There's a lot more security when you're at the dock in a slip and you know all of your neighbors and they know you. Also, some marinas have security cameras watching the docks and this gives you more security.

When you're anchored in a cove or out in the open water, you could come back to find a lot of expensive items missing, and you could even come back to find your boat missing. It has happened.

Another thing you will have to deal with when you're living on the hook is that you will have to expect that the Coast Guard and other law enforcement officials will pay you a visit from time to time—sometimes in the middle of the night.

You don't have the same rights to privacy as you do on land. They can board your boat and inspect it for legal and illegal items. You will have to show that you have all of the required equipment (and that it's in working order). You'll also need to show that your registration and all of your paperwork is in order. You will even need to provide proof that you have been getting your black and gray water legally pumped out. Don't forget that you need certain legal lights at night while you're at anchor.

As one member of our group said, "In my younger days, I lived on the hook for over a year, but now I don't think the freedom and cost savings are worth the hassle. I think paying for a slip is well worth the money."

## Mooring

There is another option that's similar to living on the hook. It's called mooring. It's basically the same as being tied to an anchor, but you are tied to a ball that's tied to a heavy, sunken concrete block. You usually have to pay a setup fee and then a small monthly fee to use the system, but it's about half the price of renting a dock at a marina.

Mooring balls are a lot stronger than your anchor, so when storms come you are a lot more secure. Many mooring fields are owned by the city or the county.

Also, your monthly mooring fee usually includes free dinghy dock privileges, showers, use of the laundry facilities at the marina, a free parking space for your car, free pump-out service for getting rid of your black and gray water, and free fresh water fill-up privileges. All of this is not always included, so be sure you know what's included in the mooring fee you will be paying.

**Bottom line:** I'm not trying to talk you out of living on the hook or mooring. I just want to make sure you know what you're getting into. Living on the hook is a free way to live, and you're more or less away from civilization, but there's a big downside.

As one member of our group said, "I lived on the hook for a couple of years. I enjoyed it. I was doing my work on my computer, so I didn't have to go to shore very often and I could go in for supplies on my schedule (when the weather and waves were favorable). I saved a lot of money, and it was a fun experience, but it was a different lifestyle. I like a more laid back lifestyle now living at a marina—even if it is more expensive."

## Chapter 8:

---

# How Much Will a Dependable Boat Cost?

---

*"Waves are not measured in feet or inches, they are measured in increments of fear."*

~ Buzzy Trent

Buying the right boat at the right price is one of the hardest, most time-consuming, most complicated, and, of course, most expensive parts of becoming a liveaboard.

I've devoted the next three chapters to this process, but before I go into all of the pitfalls to avoid, how to find the right boat, and how to negotiate the best price, I want to go over some numbers with you so you will have an idea about what kind of boat you can afford on your budget.

It's not usually a matter of whether you can afford to buy a boat or not. You're on this earth, and you have to live somewhere, and living on a boat can be one of the least expensive ways to live. If you have any cash at all (or any credit), you can buy a boat that you can live on.

I had a friend a few years ago who was living on his boat, and he was looking for someone he could give the boat to. He had tried to sell his boat, but he couldn't get anyone to buy it at any price. Obviously, his boat wasn't in very good condition, but I know it was liveable because he had been living on his boat at the marina for the last three years.

The reason he wanted to find someone to give his boat to was that he had taken a job overseas and he couldn't just walk off and leave a boat. And it's against the law to take it out to sea and sink it. He joked sometimes (at least, I think he was joking) that he wished a hurricane or a big storm would come along and then maybe he could take his boat out to sea and sink it and say that it sunk in the storm.

I know he finally sold the mast and the engine (which were about the only things on the boat that had any value), but I don't know what he ever did with his boat.

Back to how much a dependable, liveable boat would cost you.

## What Size Boat Do You Want (need)?

When you start looking at boats, they are all going to seem really small compared to the house, apartment or condo you're living in now. My advice is to go with the smallest boat that you can feel reasonably comfortable in. I've heard a lot more new liveaboards say that they wish they had a smaller boat than I've heard talking about wanting a larger boat.

The larger the boat the more expensive it is to maintain, the more expensive the slip will be and also the harder it will be to handle.

## One Other Point to Consider

Here is the advice from one member of our group. "A lot of people talk about the length of a boat, but that's not the most important measurement in my opinion. I would recommend that you get a boat that you can stand up in—maybe not in all parts of the boat but most of it. That may not be a big problem for you, but

I'm six foot three inches tall, and there are a lot of sailboats that I can't stand up in. Having to bend over all the time gets old fast. I know. I've been there."

Powerboats generally have more head room than sailboats and center-cockpit sailboats generally have more room that aft-cockpit sailboats. With sailboats, there is a tradeoff between comfort and performance.

By the way, you have to be careful with terms when you're talking about boats. The bathroom and the toilet in a boat are both referred to as the "head", but that's not the head I'm talking about here when I refer to head room. I'm talking about the one on your shoulders. Maybe I should have called that one your "noggin".

Getting back to what size of boat you need—many people say that a 28 to 33-foot boat is about the minimum size that would be comfortable as a liveaboard. For two people, that would probably be a good size to go with. One member of our group said, "I live solo on a 26-foot boat and find it to be plenty big enough for just me."

## Your Goal When Buying Your First Liveaboard is to Buy One That You Can Resale at a Profit

Unless you've done a lot of research and have looked at a lot of boats (or have a lot of experience with boats), you probably don't know enough about boats and your needs to pick out the perfect boat to start with. That's why a lot of liveaboards after two years have a different boat than they started with.

When you buy an older boat, be aware that the motor or sails are probably worn out, and the electronics are probably out of date. If any of these things have been replaced lately, that's a big plus because what they spent replacing all of these things did not increase the value of the boat nearly as much as they spent. In other words, you would be getting these items at a big discount.

Also, keep in mind that most people want a diesel engine, wheel steering, and roller furling. Having these things makes a boat a lot easier to sell.

With these facts in mind, do your research and looking, but don't worry too much about finding the boat of your dreams. Find one that you can sell at a profit in a year or two when you do find your dream boat.

The following chapters tell you how to do this.

## Where and How to Find the Best Deals on Boats

Since there are well over a million boats for sale at any given time you would think that boat builders would stop building them. With that many boats for sale, there are some real bargains out there. A lot of boat owners want to get rid of their boats and are willing to accept any reasonable offer, and many of them will even accept an unreasonable offer.

*YachtWorld* and *MarineSource* are two of the most popular places to look for boats. Below are links to their websites:

http://www.yachtWorld.com

http://marineSource.com

You can also find boats by searching CraigsList and eBay at the links below.

http://CraigsList.org

http://eBay.com

I go into details about how to find what boats actually sold for on eBay in chapter 11 and I also show you how to search CraigsList to look in other parts of the country for the kind of boat you want.

Of course, if you go with a broker, and I think you probably should, after you tell him how you plan to use the boat, what your budget is, and the things you generally like and dislike in a boat, he will have access to other sources of good used boats that you might not be aware of.

## Two Examples of the Cost of a Boat

The truth is that living on a boat can be one of the least expensive ways to live and most people can afford it on a modest income or even if their only income is their Social Security check. Yes, it CAN be inexpensive.

As my son said, "It didn't cost me much at all the years I lived on my houseboat anchored in different coves of a TVA lake. Of course, when I lived on my sailboat off the coast of Florida and spent a lot of time in marinas, things got more expensive."

Don't get me wrong, you can spend a fortune living on a boat. The old joke about a boat being a hole in the water that you throw money in can be all too true. The fact that you can (and many people do) spend a lot of money living the boating lifestyle doesn't mean that you have to.

Jason and Nikki Wynn sold their motorhome and went looking for a sailboat. They were hoping to get one they liked for about $100,000, and then they started looking at $200,000 boats. They ended up with a beautiful Catamaran for a little over $300,000. They still had to spend some money on it. They are sailing the Caribbean and enjoying their liveaboard lifestyle. You can follow their adventures at:

www.GoneWithTheWynns.com

On the other end of the scale Wayne, bought the boat he lives on for $400. He paid another $400 to get the engine running, but for $800 he has a boat that he lives on. You can learn about his story by watching this video:

https://www.youtube.com/watch?v=KKkNKEJ_Pfg

A lot of this book is about living on a much lower budget than most people think about when they think about living full time on a boat.

There are in between lifestyles also. My friends, Mark and Debbie have their liveaboard sailboat near St. Augustine, Florida. It's a 30-foot sailboat. They paid $10,000 for it and after doing a lot of work on it themselves, it's now worth about twice that.

Mark said that the key to increasing the value of a boat is to spend time and money on the interior. First impressions have a lot to do with the value of a boat. If the inside looks nice, it greatly increases the value of a boat.

If you like fun, adventure, freedom, and a stress-free lifestyle, living full time on a boat is an option worth considering, and obviously that's what you're doing and why you bought this book.

Beyond a doubt, there will be a lot of things that will go wrong when you live on a boat, so whether living on a boat is a stress-free lifestyle or not will depend on your attitude. If you let things get to you, it can be a stressful life.

For most liveaboards, the lifestyle is not all romantic. It's not sitting on the deck anchored off of some tropical island with a drink in your hand all of the time. For most boaters, life is more a matter of being tethered to land in a marina and rocking (hopefully gently) most of the time then darting off to the open water as often as possible for a few hours, days or weeks before returning to their home base.

If you do want to spend your life cruising in the Caribbean, this book gives you some information on how to do that too.

**One important point:** Several places in this book I talk about it being possible to buy a boat and sell it for more than you paid for it. Yes, it's possible. Some members of our group have done that more than once, but most people lose money when they sell a boat. The boat brokers in our group were adamant that the average newbie boat buyer would probably not end up buying a boat and making money on it.

It's a fact. Boats depreciate and unless you know enough about boats to recognize a bargain, and spend the time searching for a bargain, you will lose money when you sell your boat.

So yes, it is possible to make money on your boat when you sell it, but in order to do that you have to learn a lot about boats, do a lot of searching for bargains, and then be able to do some restoration to increase the value of the boat you bought.

Remember the most important point about selling a boat at a profit is that. . .

**"You make your money when you buy a boat—not when you sell it."**

**Bottom line:** The title of this chapter is, "How Much Will a Dependable Boat Cost?" and I know I haven't answered that question. It's like asking how much a house will cost. Read the next three chapters, and then, with the information in all four chapters, I think you can decide how much it will cost you to get a boat that will fit your needs and wants.

If you have to have a number, I would say that most liveaboards spend between $10,000 and $100,000. I know; that's a wide range. In my opinion, $20,000 to $30,000 will buy a good liveaboard boat and even $10,000 to $20,000 will buy an acceptable liveaboard. Of course, a lot of people live on boats that cost a lot more and a lot less than this.

# Chapter 9:

---

# Buyer Checklist and Pitfalls to Avoid

---

*"The man who rows the boat seldom has time to rock it."*

~ Bill Copeland

By all means hire a surveyor to check your dream boat thoroughly before you buy it. I suggest that you do this even if you feel you don't need one. If you're financing your boat, the bank or financial institution lending you the money will probably require that you hire a surveyor and provide them with a copy of his report.

You might think, *Ok, I agree. I'll hire a surveyor. Since I'm going to have a surveyor go over the boat with a fine-tooth comb, does that mean I don't need to worry too much about the condition of the boat myself?*

If you have plenty of money and time, maybe you could have a surveyor look at every boat you're considering. Otherwise you need to look at the boats you're considering as closely as you can and only hire a surveyor when you find a boat that you think you want to buy. You can make an offer on a boat subject to everything being as represented by the seller (as verified by your surveyor).

Surveyors are not cheap (and if you find one who is, he's probably not the one you want to use). If you pay a surveyor and he finds something that's a deal killer, you've lost the money you paid the surveyor, but he's saved you money in the long run because he kept you from buying a boat that has expensive problems.

## Your Job Is to Eliminate as Many Boats as Possible

Even with limited experience (and the help of the list below) you will be able to eliminate a lot of boats. And even if you don't eliminate a boat, you can find things that you can get the owner to agree to fix (or drop the price so you can get it fixed) or else you move on and don't make an offer on the boat.

Remember that, when you're looking at boats, your job is to eliminate as many as possible, so the better job you can do of eliminating boats the sooner you will find the one perfect boat—at least, one that's perfect for you and your budget right now.

When you first start looking at boats, you don't have to check every little detail. Initially, you want to see a lot of boats to get a gut-feel for the type of boat you want. But after a while you will be ready to start seriously looking at boats. That's when you will need to look at each boat you're seriously considering with the following checklist in hand.

When it comes to buying a boat, there are some things that you should consider to be deal killers. Walk away fast if you find any of these things.

Also, go with your gut. If a deal seems too good to be true or the deal just doesn't feel right or you don't have a good feeling about the owner or sales agent, walk away.

There are a lot of great boat bargains on the market right now and in this market as a buyer with cash (or pre-approved financing) you are in the driver's seat.

Later in this chapter is a list of the things you need to be sure to inspect and check off before you put a boat on your list to be seriously considered. I call these "deal killers". I have also included a checklist of other things you need to be sure to look at. These are things that you should be able to take a look at yourself.

Note that not everything has to pass, but if it doesn't and you buy the boat, you want it to be because you considered a fault or problem and decided that you could fix it or that it wasn't important to you.

What you don't want to happen is to have your surveyor find something that is a deal killer that you forgot to check.

After you have checked everything on the list and made a note of anything that is a problem, you can then look at the items on the list that are problems and decide whether they're a big enough deal to ask the owner to fix them. And, of course, you can use the problem items in your negotiating to bring the price down.

Make pictures and keep good notes as you do your searching. After you look at a few boats, the details will all start running together. Don't depend on your memory unless you are only looking at very few boats.

Armed with this checklist, you are ready to start your search. Enjoy the adventure.

There are seven things that you should probably consider to be deal killers. You might be a little more tolerant of a few of the items than some people would be, but most people don't want to deal with these problems right off the bat when they purchase a boat.

## Seven Deal Killers

1. **Signs that the boat has been submerged:** Look for any signs of rust around the engine. Rust could mean that there has been a lot of water in the area or maybe even that the boat has been submerged.

2. **A soft or rotted floor:** (Note that boaters call the floor of a boat the deck.) One of the most important (and easiest) things to check is the deck. Walk all over it and look especially at the corners. It's usually made of wood, and any sign of softness indicates rotting, and a deck is expensive to replace. If you find any sign of rotting, there's probably a lot of hidden rot that you don't see.

3. **A transom showing signs of rotting:** Be sure to take a close look at the transom. The transom is part wood and part fiberglass. If it's soft and shows sign of rotting, this is a serious problem. I would walk away.

4. **Mildew:** This is especially important to look for. Mildew can be almost impossible to get rid of when it's back inside the walls. It's also very bad for your health. You don't have to see it. If you can smell it when you first go inside the cabin, it's there. Walk away. Be sure to check when you first walk in. Your nose will adjust to it quickly, and you won't know it's there after a minute or two, so be observant when you first walk in.

5. **Has the boat been smoked in?** For some people, this is not a big deal, but for others it's a major concern and a deal killer. Be sure to also consider this when you first walk in. Like mildew, you won't be able to detect it after your nose has adjusted to the smell. By the way, if you don't think your nose will block out smells quickly, try this. Blindfold someone and then hold half of an orange, lemon or onion near their nose and ask them to identify the smell. They can almost always do this easily. Hold it there and ask them to tell you when you take it away. In a very short time, they will usually say that you have taken it away. That's how fast your nose disregards strong smells. I guess it's nature's way of saying that if there's a strong smell, and you can't do anything about it, you might as well ignore it.

6. **If you catch the owner (or agent) not being truthful with you:** If he lies about one thing, he will lie about more things. Be sure to ask a few questions that you already know the answer to in order to see if he is truthful.

7. **Engine problems:** Be sure to pull the dip stick and look for clean oil and, by all means, check the oil for water (which would be indicated by the oil looking milky).

## Checklist

Your boat may not have all of the items listed below on it, but be sure to check the items it does have to make sure they're working properly.

(**Note:** You may not even know what some of these things are, but Google the terms you're not familiar with and you will see pictures and descriptions. You'll soon be an expert—or at least more knowledgeable.)

- Generator (check to see that it cranks relatively easily and that it puts out the proper voltage under load)
- Solar panels and controller
- Water heater
- Microwave

- Refrigerator (on propane and electric)
- Furnace
- Air conditioner
- All electrical devices and all electronics
- Steering system
- Shifting system
- Propeller
- Battery (house and engine)
- Wiring connections
- Bilge pump(s)
- Fuel tank(s)
- Gauges
- Seacock(s)
- Lines (ropes)
- Windshield
- Liferail/Pulpit
- Hull finish
- Bottom surface
- Deck and cabin

- Helm station

- Hull to deck joint

- Molding trim

- Hardware

- Cushions

- Hatches

- Lights

- Mast(s)

- Boom

- Sail(s)

- Running rigging

- Standard rigging

- Keel/Centerboard

- Rudder

- Air conditioner

- Galley equipment

- Upholstery

- Water tightness (look for any leaks and check for water in the bilge)

## Take a Close Look at the Boat as a Whole

You can tell a lot from your first impression. Does it look like it's been well maintained? If the owner didn't take good care of the things you can see, more than likely he didn't take care of the things you can't see.

- When looking at the outside of the boat, is there any cracking in the fiberglass, are there signs that repair work has been done? How faded is the gel-coat and can it be restored?

- Are there any bubbles or blisters in the fiberglass? This is an expensive problem to try to fix.

- Check the rub rail for signs that it's been beaten up and check to make sure that there is no separation under the rub rail. This is a problem that's expensive to fix.

- Check the engine. Is it clean, does it look well maintained, how are the belts and hoses?

- Of course, check to make sure that all of the appliances and equipment work properly.

There are a lot of other things that your surveyor will check for, but these are the easy things that you can check and will allow you to eliminate a lot of boats and not have to pay a surveyor to look at them.

## Five Coast Guard Required Safety Items

• Life Jackets

• Sound Signaling Device, (horn, whistle, or bell)

• Fire Extinguisher

• Throwable (such as an approved floatation cushion)

• Visual Distress Signal

Since these items are required by the Coast Guard when you're out on the water, make sure that they are included and in good condition. If they're not, you're going to have to spend the money immediately to buy them. Factor that cost into what the boat is going to cost you.

**Bottom line:** Don't depend on your memory. Make a list of the things I've described above and especially the deal killer items. Make sure you check these things off as being inspected for each boat you look at. Checking for these things could keep you from buying a big problem and then having to spend a lot of money to get something fixed. It's also a good idea to take a lot of pictures of boats that you're seriously interested in.

# Seven Negotiating Tips for Boat Buyers

*"A small sailing craft is not only beautiful, it is seductive and full of strange promise and the hint of trouble."*

~ E. B. White

Boat prices are a lot more negotiable than car prices, so keep this fact in mind when you hear the initial asking price.

Some people don't like to negotiate, but in the boat market almost all prices are negotiable and not just a little bit but a lot. You can save a lot of money by doing just a little haggling. Use the simple negotiating techniques described below and you should be able to get your dream boat at a great price.

Note that not a single one of the following statements says that you won't pay the price being asked. You imply it, but you don't actually say it. You are always free to accept the price that the seller is asking.

A lot of people don't like to negotiate, but when it comes to houses, cars, and boats, you have to. Sellers expect it, and they don't quote you their best price to start with. In almost all cases, the seller (broker or individual) doesn't realistically expect you to pay their asking price.

Negotiating doesn't have to be a hassle or an unpleasant experience. Just use one or more of the seven statements below and watch the asking price start to decrease in a hurry. If you use these statements, negotiating can be a fun experience.

If you're going through a broker (even if it's your own broker instead of the seller's broker) you still want to use these negotiating techniques. You don't ever want your broker to know how much you're really willing to pay or that this is your dream boat. As the old poker saying goes, "Hold your cards close to your chest."

## Here Are My Seven All-time Favorite Negotiating Phrases for People Who Don't Like to Negotiate

### #1. ALWAYS, ALWAYS flinch at the first price or proposal.

You should almost fall over because you are so shocked. Do this even if the price you hear is way less than you expected. Flinch and say, "That's WAY out of my budget," and then **shut up**. Don't say a word. Just sit and wait for the price to drop.

### #2. Next, when you get the lower price quote, you should say, "You've got to do better than that."

And, again, you shut up. If you open your mouth, you won't get the next price concession. If you say yes to the first offer, the other person will know that they quoted you a price that was too low. They may even try to find a way to increase the price. They may say something like, "Well, let me see if the boss will go along with this price," or, "Let me make sure that this is ok with my wife."

### #3. If you make a counter offer, ALWAYS ask for a much lower price than you expect to get.

One of the cardinal rules of negotiating is that you should ask the other side for more than you expect to get. Henry Kissinger went so far as to say, "Effectiveness at the negotiating table depends upon overstating one's demands."

## #4. Never offer to split the difference.

It's human nature to want to "play fair". Our sense of fair play dictates to us that if both sides give equally, then that's fair. Realize that the other side is almost always willing to split the difference, so you should try to get a slightly better deal than that.

## #5. How to use two powerful negotiating techniques all in one sentence. The two techniques are: "Absent Higher Authority" and "If I could, would you?"

We've all experienced the "absent higher authority" technique. For example, "Our insurance regulations won't let you go back in the shop," or, "The loan committee wouldn't go along with those terms."

You don't get to talk to the loan committee (it doesn't exist), and you don't get to talk to the insurance company. It's a higher authority that you can't talk to.

Here's how to use the technique in your favor for once.

When you're down to the final negotiations, you can say, "If I could get my (financial adviser, spouse or some absent higher authority) to go along with this, you will fill the fuel tank, won't you?"

Notice that in this statement you haven't agreed to anything.

The owner or broker is in a position of feeling that they need to go along with what you're proposing to keep the deal from falling apart.

**#6. Nibble for more at the end.**

You can usually get a little bit more even after you have basically agreed on everything—if you use a technique I call nibbling.

You can say, "You ARE going to change the oil in the engine," or, "You ARE going to fix (or replace) the whatever, aren't you?"

The broker is already thinking about what he is going to do with his commission. The last thing he wants is for this sale to fall through. He will usually give just a little bit more if you "nibble".

**#7.** When you're getting close to the end of the negotiations, and everything is just about nailed down, say, **"I'm getting nervous about this," and then SHUT UP.** The other party will think the deal is about to fall apart, and they will likely throw in one more concession to seal the deal.

**Bottom line:** Use some or all of the above seven negotiating techniques and you will walk away with a boat at way less than the going rate. If you can buy your boat at way less than the fair market value, you will stand a good chance of being able to sell your boat and make a profit when and if you decide you want a different boat.

# Chapter 11

# How to Buy a Boat and Not Get Burned

*"Ships are the nearest things to dreams that hands have ever made."*

~ Robert N. Rose

I assume by now that you're about ready to buy your boat. Finding the right boat and buying it is a fun, exciting and scary process. The purpose of this chapter is to leave the fun and exciting part of the process intact and take out the scary part.

This chapter is long, but it needs to be. There's a lot of information you need to know in order to buy a good boat and not get burned. More than likely you already know some of this information, but bear with me as I cover the basic information that new boat buyers may not know, and I bet experienced boaters will find some nuggets here too.

Below is a list of the nine steps you need to go through when buying a boat.

## Nine Steps to Buying a Boat

1. Decide what type of boat you want.

2. Decide how much you can afford to spend on a boat.

3. Does the type of boat you want match your budget?

4. Get your cash freed up or your financing pre-approved.

5. Decide if you should you use a broker.

6. Look at a LOT of boats.

7. Get a surveyor to inspect the boat after your offer is accepted.

8. Buy insurance.

9. Close the deal and take delivery.

Now let's go over each one of these nine steps in detail.

## Decide What Type of Boat You Want

The first thing you need to decide is whether you want a sailboat or a powerboat. It's like considering whether you want a dog or a cat. It's a personal preference. From an emotional standpoint, most people have a pretty good idea about whether they want a sailboat or a powerboat, but if you need a little help from a logical standpoint, here are some facts.

- A powerboat is generally more comfortable and livable than a sailboat.

- A sailboat is slow, quiet and there are no fuel costs necessary to go places.

- A powerboat can be very expensive to operate if you cruise a lot.

- A powerboat is more expensive to maintain.

- It takes a lot more training and skill to operate a sailboat.

- A sailboat has more stability in rough water (and even in the marina).

- Powerboats are generally faster than sailboats.

- Powerboats can pretty much go somewhere on a schedule.

- Sailboats go with the wind. How long and IF they get somewhere depends on the wind.

- Sailboats come with center cockpit and aft cockpit designs. Which one do you like better?

### Fiberglass vs. wood

I'll make that decision easy for you. Go with fiberglass. The only good thing about wooden boats is that they're cheap. A wooden boat might work for you if you're just going to keep it in the marina and not go anywhere— and if you're going to be paying cash. It's hard to get financing and insurance for older wooden boats. If you buy a wooden boat, make sure you like it because you will probably have a hard time selling it.

### Size does matter when it comes to boats

In my opinion, most people buy a boat that's too big. The bigger the boat the harder it is to handle and the more expensive it is for just about everything you do to it. Slip rental, hauling the boat out of the water, cleaning the bottom, and you name it, everything about a boat is charged for by the foot.

Also, if a sailboat is very large, it will take two people to sail it. If you plan to do any sailing by yourself, make sure you buy a boat that can be handled by one person, and, of course, make sure you have the strength and skill to handle it.

Longer boats have more living and storage space and are more comfortable, so weigh all of the pros and cons when deciding on the type of boat that would be best for you.

Some people think of houseboats and liveaboard pontoon boats as another type of boat, and in a way they are, but in my opinion they are just different variations of a powerboat. One member of our group said, "I used to live on a 44-foot houseboat, but now I prefer the excitement of a liveaboard sailboat—even though it does have less room."

Don't think of the process of deciding which type of boat is right for you as being a frustrating process. Enjoy the excitement and adventure.

## Decide How Much You Can Afford to Spend on a Boat

The next step for most people in the boat buying process is to run the numbers and find out how much they can afford to spend on a boat. Many people mistakenly think that they have to buy the most expensive boat they can afford.

Of course, the first number you need to know is how much cash you have readily available and how much more you can put your hands on with a little time and effort. For example, can you sell one of your cars, and what other assets do you have that you can turn into cash? After all, you will need to get rid of a lot of your stuff before you move onto a boat.

Lenders generally want 20% down, and they want you to have a debt to income ratio of no more than about 40%. In other words, no more than 40% of your income should be going to paying off credit card debt, car payment, home mortgage or rent, etc.

Of course, you will need to have a steady job, and you will need to provide two years of tax records proving that your income is what you say it is. Most boat loans are for 15 years (sometimes up to 20 years for boats selling for $75,000 or more).

To get an idea of how much your boat payments will be, search Google for "Loan Calculator" and you will find several websites with tools that will allow you to enter the amount to be financed, the interest rate (which is about 5% to 6% right now) and the term of the loan, and it will show you your monthly payments.

For example, if you planned to buy a boat in the $40,000 range and put 20% down, you would be financing $32,000, and at 5% for 15 years your payments would be $253 a month.

**One word of caution:** Don't spend all of your cash on a down payment. Boats are notorious for having things break that require cash to repair. And of course, you'll need money for living expenses, renting a slip at a marina, renting a storage unit, moving expenses, and money for a lot of other things that will add up.

Don't run out of cash just to get a fancier boat than you can comfortably afford. It's the lifestyle that's enjoyable, not the size of boat you have. Having a nicer or bigger boat won't make you happier—well, maybe a little bit.

By knowing how much cash you have access to and how much money you can borrow, you have answered the question of how much you can afford to spend on a boat. Of course, knowing how much you can afford doesn't mean that you should actually spend that much.

## Does the Type of Boat You Want Match Your Budget?

Now that you know the price range of boats you should be looking at and whether you want a sailboat or a powerboat, you're ready to start actually looking at some boats. Start by looking online because that way you can see a lot of boats with very little effort.

The four places you should look first are:

- YachtWorld.com

- MarineSource.com

- CraigsList.org

- eBay.com

On these sites, you can see lots of boats and lots of pictures. Best of all, you can get an idea of what prices sellers are asking for the kinds of boats you're interested in. Keep in mind that the prices you see are asking prices and almost all boats sell for less (sometimes a lot less) than the asking price.

## How to find the actual prices that boats recently sold for

Knowing what boats like the one you're considering buying actually sold for recently will help you decide if that boat is within the price range you can afford.

When you engage the services of a broker, they have access to information on YachtWorld.com that the general public doesn't have. They can see what a particular boat sold for, where it was located and the condition of the boat. In other words, they have a vast database of what boats like the one you're looking for have recently sold for.

Another way to get a good idea of what boats are selling for is to check out eBay. Be sure to look at the "Completed listings" to see what boats actually sold for. Sometimes the starting bid or the reserve price is way out of line, and the boat will not sell.

To view the "Completed listings" and see the actual price boats sold for, log into your eBay account and then, in the top right corner of your screen, in small print (just to the right of the big blue "Search" box), you will see the word, "Advanced." Click on this link and then enter the keyword, "sailboat or powerboat." Scroll down and click on the "Completed listings" box and below that enter a price range or at least enter a minimum price. If you don't enter a minimum price, you will see 20,000 items including anchors, lights and everything that has the word "boat" in the listing.

Then click on the blue "Search" box. This will take you to the list of completed auctions. The prices shown in green are the ones that sold.

I think you will be pleasantly surprised at how little some of these boats sold for.

Another way to compare boat prices (and find bargains) is to search CraigsList.org in areas other than just in or near your city. You can use the Search Tempest website at the link below. The program will search for the type of boat you enter into the search box and search within the number of miles from your zip code (or any other zip code that you enter), which you select. Here is the link to their website:

http://www.searchtempest.com

You can also search by keyword and price. For example, if you wanted to find all of the sailboats priced between $20,000 and $30,000 that are within 400 miles of your zip code (or another zip code) you can do that at this site.

## How to Handle the Gap in Price Between What You Want and What You Can Afford

Now that you have a general idea about what kind of boat you can get for what price and you have an idea of what kind of boat you like and will fit your lifestyle, the next step is to go back and look at your budget again. More than likely you will find that there's a gap between what you want and what you can afford (or at least, what you want to spend).

This is sometimes called having champagne taste and beer money.

Don't give up. You may be able to find the boat that fits your needs for 20% to 40% less than the fair market retail value. Don't be afraid to make a low-ball offer. Sometimes you can get a boat for 50% less than the asking price but don't count on it. Knowing these facts should put a lot more boats back into your budget.

**There are three ways to handle the problem of wanting a higher priced boat than your budget will allow**

1. **The best way to handle the problem is to do more homework, legwork, and negotiating to find a real bargain.** There are bargains out there. The old saying that you get what you pay for is not always true when it comes to boats. You can get ripped off and pay way too much, but you can also end up with a great deal on your boat and pay way less than the fair market value. Don't ignore boat dealers and brokers. They usually have their used boats priced at a high retail price, but they will negotiate big time. I know of one case where a dealer sold a used boat for less than half of what he was asking for it. Don't be afraid to make a very low-ball offer. If you have the cash (or pre-approved financing) and are ready to buy today, dealers will make some pretty big concessions—particularly on older boats that they have had for a while.

2. **Another way to handle the problem is to change your wants.** This is not as bad an option as you might think. The price of the boat you end up with will not have much to do with how happy you are living the liveaboard lifestyle. I see people all the time who have very expensive boats and they don't seem nearly as happy as people who have a low-priced boat that they have customized, decorated, and given character. Go back and look at some of the lower priced boats and think about what you can do with them to make them feel like home. And keep in mind that you can always sell the boat you start out with (maybe even at a profit) and then buy a different one after you've lived the liveaboard lifestyle for a while and know what you really want.

3. **A third way to get the more expensive boat you want is to liquidate as many of your assets as you possibly can.** This helps in two ways. Take the cash and pay off as much debt as possible. Having more cash for a larger down payment and also having a lower debt to income ratio will allow you to finance a much more expensive boat. One technique a lot of people do is to sell their high-priced car and totally eliminate the payments. You can pay cash for an older, low-priced car (which may be all you need) and then buy a more expensive car later after you

get your boat and decide that you want, need, and can afford a higher priced car. Of course, if you have two cars and can possibly get by with just one (even temporarily), sell your second car.

## Get Your Cash Freed up or Your Financing Pre-approved

Boat brokers will take you a lot more seriously if you have cash or pre-approved financing, but you don't want to go start applying for boat loans just yet. There are two reasons why you don't want to do this. First, financial institutions want some idea of the general type of boat they will be financing, and you will need that information to put on your application. The second reason is that every time you apply for a loan and get turned down, it lowers your credit score.

So, when you're ready to apply for a loan, talk to the bank and explain your situation, your debts, income, etc. and get a pretty good idea of whether or not you'll be approved for the loan before you actually formally apply.

My recommendation is, unless you've lived on a boat before and know exactly what kind of boat you want, don't buy the most expensive boat you can afford. Buy a boat much less than you can afford. Make sure it has good bones and you can fix it up and add extras to it later or sell it and buy another boat when you know more about what you can afford.

You don't have to keep up with the Joneses. You might be a lot happier taking the $20,000 cash you have and buying a $20,000 boat to start with than you would be using that cash as a down payment on a $100,000 boat. It's something to think about. Being debt-free makes living on a boat a lot less stressful and more enjoyable. You can always move up to a bigger boat later.

One last point: When you're living around a marina and talking to other boat owners, it's a lot easier to run into real bargains than it is just to go out cold turkey looking at boats.

## Should You Use a broker?

The simple and short answer is, "Yes." Having a good broker is extremely important if you're new to boating, but even if you're an experienced boater and have bought and sold several boats, I would still recommend using your own broker. If you are buying a relatively low-cost boat and you are knowledgeable about boats, you could skip the broker, but in most cases, you would be better off with a broker.

The seller will most likely have a broker, but he is representing the seller's best interest, and no matter how friendly he seems, he is not looking out for your interest.

## Having Your Own Broker Won't Cost You a Dime. His Fee Is Paid by the Seller

When you have your own broker, the commission the seller will pay (usually, 10%) will be split between two brokers. Actually, the seller's broker is the one who loses in this arrangement because he only gets half of the commission he would have received if you didn't have a broker. Of course, he won't have to do as much work because your broker will be doing some of the legwork.

A good, knowledgeable broker can save you a lot of money and steer you away from a boat that's not right for you.

**Note:** You have to engage your broker and have him show you boats. After the owner or the seller's broker has shown you a boat, you can't bring your broker into the deal at this point.

If you're buying a boat from an individual who is not using a broker, it will be written into the contract that the seller will be paying your broker's commission. In other words, the seller will know that he will only be getting 90% of what you're offering. Don't worry about the details. Your broker will be writing the contract, and you can be sure that he will look out for his commission.

If you ask the seller's broker a question, he can't legally lie to you, but if you don't ask, he may decide not to mention some bad things he knows about a boat.

It's important that you spend some time selecting a knowledgeable broker that you like and feel good about. Get recommendations from marina owners and managers, ask other boat owners, and, by all means, find out if the broker you're considering is a member of one of the major broker associations in the United States. Some of the broker associations with high standards that I recommend are:

- Yacht Brokers Association of America

- California Brokers Association

- Florida Brokers Association

There are others, but do your homework and make sure that you will be dealing with an ethical and professional broker.

## Look at a LOT of Boats

Before you start looking at boats in person, do a lot of online searches, read reviews, check prices, and try to get a general idea of what type and size boat you're looking for. And know what the fair market price is for that boat. You can't recognize a bargain if you don't know what a particular boat is worth.

When you do start looking at boats, you have to change your mind set about what is considered a small living space. When you compare any boat (except multi-million dollar yachts) to the living space you're used to, it is inevitably going to seem extremely small. This comparison may lead you to look at (and maybe even buy) a boat that is way bigger than you need.

When you first step inside the living quarters of the boats you'll be looking at, your first impression will probably be, "My gosh (or something stronger), that's the smallest living space I've ever seen. I had more room than that in my first Boy Scout tent."

Yea, living on a boat takes some getting used to and a change of attitude about how much space you really need.

A bigger boat is not only more expensive to buy but also more expensive to maintain and more difficult to handle and maneuver. You'll probably realize this after living on a boat for a year or so. By then you might realize that you made an expensive mistake if you bought a big boat.

Be sure to discuss your wants, needs, and budget with your broker and tell him your ideas about how you plan to use your boat and let him help you select the type and size of boats you should be looking at.

When you're looking at boats, one of your main goals should be to eliminate as many as possible. If every boat you look at is still on your maybe list, you will soon have 100+ boats that you're considering. That's impossible to deal with.

I would recommend that for your first liveaboard you consider an older fiberglass boat and, by old, I mean maybe 20 or 30 years old or older. Look for a boat with good bones. You can fix everything else.

When it comes to buying and owning a boat, there are two quotes from Warren Buffett you should keep in mind:


*"Price is what you pay. Value is what you get."*
~ Warren Buffett

*"Should you find yourself in a chronically leaking boat, energy devoted to changing vessels is likely to be more productive than energy devoted to patching leaks."*

~ Warren Buffett

When you start looking at boats, be sure to take notes and, make pictures and videos of the boats you're seriously interested in. In your notes be sure to include a lot of information such as location, price, things that are wrong with the boat, the basic facts like the length of the boat, what equipment is included, and the asking price.

Believe me; you won't have to look at many boats before they all start running together in your head.

Be sure to ask if there is anything or any equipment on board that will not be included in the purchase. Also, by making pictures and videos, you will have proof of what was on the boat when you were told that everything was included. Include videos of the owner or broker describing the boat and what's included.

Keep in mind that buying a boat could be only the tip of the iceberg when it comes to the money you will be spending. Of course, it doesn't have to be that way. The two things that could end up costing you a lot of money are repairs and adding equipment.

When you're looking at boats, there may be some obvious things that stand out as needing repairs, but a lot of things may not show up until you have a surveyor look at the boat and give you a report. When you make an offer on a boat, it will always be based on everything being in good working order (unless it was stated to be otherwise) and subject to verification by your surveyor. You don't want to spend money hiring a surveyor until after your offer is accepted.

The second area where you may end up spending a lot of money is on adding equipment to the boat. Of course, the more equipment the boat has the less you will need to spend. What equipment you will need will depend on your intended use of the boat. Are you just going to mainly live on your boat in the marina and only take it out occasionally, are you going to sail a lot but mostly in intercoastal waterways or are you planning on doing a lot of blue water sailing?

One other option is that you could buy your boat and add the equipment you need over time as your budget allows.

As was stated before, when looking at a boat, be sure to make a note of what equipment it has (and if it's working properly). Below is a partial list of things to look for. (Note that some of the items in the list will only be needed for a sailboat and some of the items will only be necessary if you're not going to be at a marina and connected to shore power.)

- Required Coast Guard safety gear

- GPS

- VHF radio

- Anchor

- Solar panels

- Sails

- Generator

- Inverter

- Wind vane

- Windlass

- Lifeboat

- Dingy and motor

Having spare parts and duplicate equipment will be useful too, especially things like a spare bilge pump, handheld VHF radio, handheld GPS, tools, etc.

All of the items on this list are things that you may want or need sooner or later, and if they're included with the boat when you buy it, you'll be getting them for almost nothing.

The general consensus among boaters is that searching for a boat is like searching for a spouse. When you find the right one, you'll know it. But just like your spouse, the boat you fall in love with won't be perfect. It will have flaws. The good news is that, unlike your spouse, most of the things that you don't like about your boat can be changed.

Each day, after looking at a few boats, spend some time back home going over your notes and pictures. Get on your computer and search on YachtWorld, MarineSource, eBay, and CraigsList and compare the price and condition of the boats that you saw that day with similar boats that you find online. This will help you discover bargains and also keep you from paying way too much for the boat you fell in love with.

As I said before, one of your main jobs, when you're looking at boats, is to eliminate as many as possible.

After doing a lot of looking, if you decide that you want a certain kind of boat (such as an Island Packet or a Comanche or a Hans Christian or an O'Day) that will make your searching a lot easier. And if you nail it down to the size you want (such as 28-feet or 34-feet) that really makes your job (and your broker's job) a lot easier.

Don't worry if you don't get the boat you fall in love with. There are over a million used boats for sale at any one time and more coming on to the market every day. There will be a better deal come along tomorrow. As the old country song says, "*There's more pretty girls than one.*" This applies to boats too.

Enjoy your search and don't limit your searching to one small area. Boats can be moved, but be sure to factor in the cost of relocating a boat when you're comparing boats.

## Get a Surveyor to Inspect the Boat

After you make an offer and have it accepted, you will need to get a competent and trustworthy surveyor to do a thorough inspection of the boat you're considering. Your broker can help you select a good surveyor. A good surveyor will find things wrong with almost any boat. That's the nature of boats. He may find something that's a deal killer for you, but more than likely he will only find minor things.

Surveyors are expensive, so you don't want to hire one before you've done your negotiations and agreed to a price for your dream boat and had your offer accepted.

The price you're willing to pay is based on the representation of the owner (or his broker) that everything is in good condition and in working order or as described.

Your broker will be able to give you an idea about how expensive the things will be to fix that the surveyor finds. The things the surveyor finds will be useful to you in your negotiations.

After all, you made your offer based on everything being in good condition (except the things you were told were not working). If you find out that some things are not as you were led to believe, you can negotiate to have the owner fix those things or make a price concession so you can have the things fixed.

If you don't come to an agreement, the money you spent on a surveyor will just be lost, and you will have to hire him (or another surveyor) again when you decide on another boat. The good news is that if you decided not to buy a particular boat because of what the surveyor found, he probably saved you a ton of money down the road.

The price the surveyor will charge you will be based on the length of the boat. He will be examining just about everything. He'll look inside the cabin, look at the topside, look at the cockpit, and check out the engine, the rigging, the water supply, and electrical system. He will take it out for a cruise (whether it's a sailboat or a powerboat) and then he will haul it out of the water and examine the bottom.

This is a lot of work and expense, but it's well worth it to make sure you're getting what you're paying for. Don't buy a boat without getting a survey.

## Buying Insurance

If you're financing your boat, you will have to have insurance and a lot of marinas require insurance, so more than likely you will need to get insurance on your boat. Here are some things to keep in mind about insurance:

- Insurance is generally much higher for liveaboards than for non-liveaboards.

- Many insurance policies have a "use clause" with things like how far off shore you can go, etc.

- Some insurance companies won't insure older boats or wooden boats.

- For larger boats, some insurance companies want to know that you have experience operating the size and type of boat they're insuring.

- Almost all insurance companies require a survey.

Don't buy a boat (or agree to buy a boat) and then find out that you can't get insurance for it. When you make an offer on a boat, make it subject to you being able to get acceptable insurance and financing.

## Closing the Deal and Taking Delivery

When it comes to the closing, that's where your broker really comes in handy. I think there are more papers to deal with and more little things that need to be done when you're buying a boat than there are when you're closing on a house.

One of the little things that's different about the paperwork necessary to buy a boat that's not required for buying a house is that a boat has a "name". Of course, you can change the name later, and that's not a big deal. A car has a VIN (vehicle identification number), but a boat has a name, and it has to be on the paperwork.

There's even a "Preferred Ship Mortgage" form—yep, you're buying a ship.

Be sure to read every word of every document. Your broker will probably do this for you, but it doesn't hurt for you to do it too. For example, sometimes, in the bank's preprinted forms, it will say something about the fact that the boat will not be used for any commercial purposes, and it will not be used as the principal dwelling for you or anyone else. What a minute. That's why you're buying the boat. If this is in the paperwork, point it out to the bank and then mark through it and initial it.

By the way, make sure the bank or lending institution you're dealing with knows up front that you're going to be living on the boat.

Most banks want to make sure the boat is properly registered with the Coast Guard. This makes the boat a U.S.-registered vessel and it makes the boat a lot easier for them to repossess in case you stop making payments and sail off into the wild blue yonder.

If you're paying cash for your boat there will be less paperwork, but there will still be a lot, and it all has to be done correctly. Sometimes there is even a requirement that you post a notice in the cabin identifying the owner of the boat and list the name of the mortgagee.

**Bottom line:** There's a lot of information in this chapter, and you will probably want to go over it again when you get closer to actually buying your boat.

Don't let all of my comments about paperwork scare you. When it's time to close on your boat, your broker will take care of all of this for you.

When it's time to close on your boat, your job at this point is to find a good bottle of champagne and plan where you're going to take your boat on its maiden voyage—even if it's just around the harbor.

# Chapter 12

# What about Pets?

*"And those who were dancing were thought to be insane by those who could not hear the music."*

~ Friedrich Nietzsche

Pets make great company and they don't take up much room (at least the little ones don't), so a lot of liveaboards have pets.

I don't have a pet now, but I've had both cats and dogs in the past. I'm more of a dog person, but I have to admit that cats are more practical for a liveaboard. The big difference is that you have to get back to the boat every few hours if you have a dog (unless you've trained him to do his business in a special place on the boat, and this is necessary if you're cruising).

If you have a cat, you can be gone all day or even for more than a day, and they're fine. Of course, they may have an attitude when you get back if they've been left for very long.

When it comes to whether a dog or a cat is the better pet for a liveaboard, facts are not going to make anyone give up their dog and get a cat or vice versa.

Pets need four things—food, water, exercise and a place to do their business. Solving the food part is pretty easy, but if you're cruising, make sure to keep a good supply of the pet's food on hand. The brand your pet is used to may not be available at every port—even if it's a common or name brand. Changing a pet's food combined with a rocking boat could be a problem for you and your pet.

Keeping water in the water bowl could be a problem if you're cruising. Just pay attention to it and add water as necessary.

There's not room on a boat for a dog or a cat to get much exercise, so guess what, you and your pet need to take walks on a regular basis.

There's no standard way to handle the "doing his business" part of having a pet on a boat. I've seen a lot of unique and creative ways. Mostly it depends on your pet and what works for him. Most techniques require some training.

Dealing with kitty litter can be a problem on a boat, and it's really a problem when you're cruising. You can't keep kitty litter in a litter box. It gets all over the boat.

Some people take their pets for walks (even cats can be trained to walk on a leash—well, most of them, anyway). The problem with this technique is that when you leave the marina for a weekend or a few days, it's hard to explain to your pet that the rules and procedures will be different for the next few days.

My brother's dog would blow a gasket before he would do anything on the boat, so when they were living on the hook for a few days at a time, twice a day my brother had to put the dog in the dinghy and row him to shore for a walk and to do his business.

There are no easy solutions for how to take care of pets when you're living on a boat, but a lot of liveaboards have a pet or two, so, for sure, there are ways to make it work. Pets have different personalities, so you just have to see what the two of you can work out.

A few pets never adjust or get sea sick. When they get sea sick, it's not enjoyable for the pet or the owner, but most pets adjust quickly. Pets make wonderful companions on a boat and many people feel that the joys of having a pet are well worth the hassles involved.

It doesn't matter what's practical. It's a personal choice.

Pets really do make great companions when traveling and living the liveaboard lifestyle. They enjoy checking out new places and seeing new things. Even cats that stay on the boat all of the time seem to enjoy and be intrigued by the new scenery.

Almost all marinas allow pets. There are some rules that must be followed, so make sure you and your pet both read the rules. They are usually straightforward, common sense rules such as no barking and your dog must be on a leash when walking on the dock or anywhere on the marina property, clean up after your pet, etc.

## Things to Be Aware of When Traveling with Your Pet

- Pay attention to the temperature in your boat when you're away. Don't let it get too hot or too cold.

- Have someone check to make sure your dog doesn't bark when you're away. Do this a few times until you're sure he is not barking while you're gone.

- Check to make sure your dog or cat doesn't decide to do damage while you're away, such as chewing or scratching on things. Some pets (especially when they're young) will tear up things when they get bored, scared or unhappy about being left. So keep a close eye on them until you know how they will act when you're away. It may be necessary to keep them in a cage while you're away.

- Put a leash on your pet when you're sailing. With the boat heeled over at a steep angle, a pet can easily fall overboard. I've even seen pets fall overboard when the boat is in the slip at the marina. I've seen pets wearing little life jackets when they're out on the deck. This gives them more freedom than being on a leash.

- Make sure your animal gets plenty of exercise. It's a good way for you to get some exercise too. Since there is not as much room for your pet to run around on a boat as there is in his yard or in your home, plan on taking him for more and longer walks than you normally do. Walking your dog around the marina is a great way to meet your neighbors. Most cats can even be trained to walk on a leash. If you start when they are kittens, it's a lot easier. Older cats sometime have a mind of their own.

- What do you do about a vet? First of all, be sure to keep current copies of all of your pet's vaccinations or you might end up getting duplicate and unnecessary treatments. One solution if you're cruising near the US coast is to use a national chain of vets such as Banfield Pet Hospital. They have offices all over the country. Go to their website at BanfieldPetHospital.com and enter the zip code where you are and you can find their closest office. Many of their offices are located in PetSmart stores. They have a centralized database, and your pet's records can be brought up at any of their offices. Of course, if you're staying in one marina, your pet will have the same local vet all the time.

- If you're on a tight budget and don't already have a pet, think twice about getting one. Owning a pet can wreak havoc with a budget. One member of our group just spent $1,800 for emergency surgery for his dog. Another member just spent over $5,000 for surgery on her cat. These kinds of unexpected expenses can wreak havoc with a tight budget.

**Bottom line:** Most pets make great traveling companions. You just have to pay a little bit of attention to their special needs (and personalities). One thing I would suggest is that if you don't presently have a pet, consider not getting one for now. Later, after you've adjusted to the liveaboard lifestyle, there will be time to consider whether you want a pet on the boat.

Of course, if you do have a dog now, take him aboard and make him your first mate. If you have a cat, he'll think he's the captain and that everything should be done to please him.

# Chapter 13:

---

# What about Children?

---

*"To have a huge, friendly whale willingly approach your boat and look you straight in the eye is without doubt one of the most extraordinary experiences on the planet."*

~ Mark Carwardine

Most children adapt to the liveaboard lifestyle quickly, the younger the better.

People are always asking me, "What about kids?" My answer is, "I suggest you keep them." Of course, you probably want a more serious answer, so I'll get on with it.

In my experience, I find that kids adjust well to the liveaboard lifestyle. They experience so much more of life and the real world than they do living in a typical neighborhood.

It's a different life for the kids, so you need to discuss it with them. They will experience a lot more of the world (even if you never leave the marina), but they may not have as much time with their current friends. With the internet, Skype, Facebook, etc. they can stay in touch with these friends and have so many interesting adventures to share with them. If they're cruising, some kids even start their own blog so their friends can keep up with them.

Of course, if you are staying in a marina, and the kids are still going to the same schools, they will be spending a lot of time with some of their existing friends.

I've found that kids meet a lot of new friends in the marinas and when cruising. They become a lot more outgoing.

I know of a family with two teenage daughters who spent two years sailing around the world, and the teenagers loved it. They were a lot more isolated than being in a marina and it didn't bother them at all. In fact, they said it was the greatest experience of their lives.

Every parent that I have talked to who is living on a boat with kids says that the kids love it. The problem with this observation is that I don't think it's necessarily a representative sample. The parents of kids who found that their kids didn't like the lifestyle are probably no longer at the marina, so I didn't get to meet them.

If you or your children are unsure about whether they would like it, you should all commit to giving it a one-year trial. A few weeks or even a few months is not long enough to really adjust and know for sure if everyone would be happy with the lifestyle.

Agree that after one year you will all sit down and discuss the whole situation and then decide whether to continue or not. In fact, I recommend that even if you don't have kids, you should sit down with your spouse every year and decide if you're both really enjoying the adventure and want to continue. I know one woman who was reluctant to move onto a boat but agreed to do it for one year because her husband wanted to so much. After the year, she was more enthusiastic about continuing than he was.

If you're cruising with kids, you will have to do home-schooling, but, in my opinion, that's so much better than subjecting kids to what goes on in traditional public schools.

Personal Note: I was talking to my six-year-old cousin the other day. She is being home-schooled, and she is in the second grade. I asked her how long it took her to do her homework every day and she said, "It normally takes me about two hours, but sometimes it takes longer if I spend too much time looking out the window."

I told her, "I know how you feel. Some days I get a lot accomplished and some days I must be spending too much time looking out the window because it takes me longer to get things done." At the age of six she has already figured out what it took me years to learn—that is, if you want to get something done, don't spend too much time looking out the window. Of course, when you're cruising or even living at a marina, many times there's so much to see when you look out the window that it's hard to resist.

## It's Important for Each Child to Have Their Own Space

In addition to having their own bed, it's important for each child to have a special place to store personal stuff. It will have to be a small space, but having one's own place is just as important as having one's own room at home. Some families find that it works great for each kid to have a small backpack to store their stuff in. Personal space is important. It doesn't have to be big, but it does need to be entirely the child's space.

If you're cruising with teenagers (or moving to a marina that's not near where they live now) it may be a little more difficult to make them happy about leaving their friends back home. Some things that help are to involve the older kids in deciding where to go if you're cruising. Even if you're not cruising, let them select and plan the next weekend trip. Also, let them learn how to do everything on the boat and (depending on their ages) let them sail the boat and do as many chores as possible. It might surprise you how fast they learn things.

Another thing that older kids enjoy from time to time is having one or two of their friends go along for a week or weekend. If there is not room on the boat for an extra person you could try what one family did, they solved the problem by letting their two kids alternate their schedule. One kid would go spend a week with Grandma and Grandpa, and the other kid would get to bring a friend on board for a week (or a weekend). Later, the other kid would go visit the grandparents and his sibling would get to bring a friend on board. Both kids enjoyed both adventures.

**Bottom line:** Letting children experience the liveaboard lifestyle is one of the best things you could do for them. The kids I've talked to who are liveaboards love their lifestyle. Just ask them where they've been, where they're going next or what they've been doing and watch their eyes light up and you will see how excited and happy they are.

Ask them to tell you about their boat if you want them to really start talking. You'll find that many of them will know more about their boat and know more about sailing than a lot of liveaboards in the marina.

# Chapter 14

# How to Live on a Boat on Your Social Security

*"Happiness is when reality is better than expectations. Sometimes you don't have much control over reality, but you always have control over your expectations."*

~ Unknown

Being able to live on a boat on just your Social Security income is easy. All you have to do is get your living expenses lower than your Social Security income. Yea, right. That's easier said than done.

Seriously, it can be done and fairly easily. Let's start at the beginning. How much will you receive each month from Social Security? If you're already getting your Social Security, you know the amount.

If you're not drawing your Social Security yet and are impatient and just want a ballpark number, here it is. The government reports that, **as of January 2017, the average retired person receiving a Social Security check gets $1,362 a month**. You may receive more than this or less. (That makes sense. That's why it's called an average.) If you want to know exactly how much you will be receiving, keep reading.

If you're not drawing your Social Security yet and want to know more about how much you will be drawing when you start receiving your benefits, I'll try to make this as short and painless as possible.

The first step in finding out if you can comfortably live the liveaboard lifestyle on your Social Security income is to find out how much income you will have to work with.

If you haven't started drawing your payments yet, let me show you how to quickly and easily find out how much you will be drawing.

Then you will know how much you have to work with, and we can work and plan from there.

## Do You Qualify to Draw Social Security?

The first thing to do is to make sure you qualify to receive Social Security benefits based on your own work. This is one of the few straightforward answers in the Social Security rule book. To receive Social Security benefits, you must have worked for at least 40 quarters during your lifetime (and earned $1,220 or more in each quarter—indexed to today's numbers). By the way, if you worked for 10 years straight, that would be 40 quarters.

The 40 quarters do not have to be consecutive. These 40 quarters have to be where Social Security Payroll taxes (also known as FICA) were deducted. Of course, you also have to be at least 62 years old before you can start receiving your benefits.

To find out exactly how much your Social Security benefits will be, you can either go to your local Social Security office (plan on being there for an hour or two) or you can go to the government website at http://www.ssa.gov/myaccount and set up your account. This will only take a few minutes.

You may get slightly different numbers by using the online tool vs. going to the Social Security office in person, but the numbers will be pretty close.

Both of these options will take some time and you may not want to stop and do either one of them right this minute, so let's go on with some general information.

After you've worked enough to qualify for Social Security benefits, your spouse (and your ex-spouse) may be able to receive Social Security benefits too. How much they receive will be based on your work record, but it will not change how much you receive in any way.

Now that you know how much you will be receiving from Social Security, the next step is to see if you can live on a boat on that income. Let's look at the numbers and I think you will be pleasantly surprised to find out that in most cases, yes, you can live on a boat on your Social Security.

## Now That You Know Your Social Security Income, Can You Be a Liveaboard on That Income?

If your Social Security income is anywhere near the national average of $1,362 per month, it will be easy, and even if your income is less than $1,000 a month, it can still be done. I know liveaboards who get by fine on less than $800 a month.

In fact, one member of our group said, "I was living on the hook for a year; my expenses were way less than

$800 a month. I didn't spend much on maintenance during that time. I ate a lot of fish that I caught, and I socialized with friends and drank a beer or two every now and then. It was a good life. I also got a lot of work done on my consulting projects during that time since I had a lot of uninterrupted time."

In chapter three, I covered how much it would typically cost to live on a boat, and you can see that it can be done for way less than the average Social Security income of $1,362 a month. Keep in mind that this is assuming that you are not paying mortgage payments on a boat. Only buy a boat that you can afford to pay cash for. You can get a liveaboard boat for well under $10,000.

But it gets even better. If you're retired and living on your Social Security and living on a boat, you have some free time—maybe for the first time in your life. You can use that free time to do something interesting and make some extra money.

If your Social Security income is covering your living expenses, just a little extra income will work wonders for your budget. Even $200 to $500 a month of extra income will change your lifestyle from just getting by to really living. With the extra income, you can go out to eat more, buy new toys (fishing equipment, new computers), take trips, buy new things for your boat, etc.

## Five Ways to Make Extra Money While Living on a Boat

The good news is that it has never been easier to make extra money while living on your boat. Here's a list of ways other liveaboards are making extra money:

1. **Write books and sell them on Amazon.** I have written several books. Some of them make over $1,500 a month for me, and some of them don't do very well. Maybe this one will be a big seller. I have friends who make over $4,000 a month from a single novel, and they have several novels that sell well. Novels sell a lot better than how-to books. The title and the cover have a lot to do with how well a book sells. There's zero cost to get Amazon to publish both the eBook version and the printed version. You can hire people on Fiverr.com to design the cover and do the proofreading and formatting for you for very little cost. You can write a book, so get started on it.

2. **Do part-time work at the marina or do maintenance work for other liveaboards.** There's always a demand for this type of work if you're handy with tools.

3. **Post videos on YouTube and monetize them.** Post videos on YouTube and select the "Monetization" option. This means that YouTube will place ads on the website with your video and then pay you for ad clicks.

If you don't see this Monetization option when you upload your video, it means that you have not linked your Google Ad Sense account to your YouTube account. That's easy to do as long as you have used the same email address for both accounts.

YouTube will pay you about $1,000 for every 100,000 clicks. That comes out to about one cent per click. It depends on the topic. I haven't done much with YouTube, but I do have one video that has had over 115,000 views. I need to get busy and put up a bunch more videos.

Some people make more than a million dollars a month from their YouTube videos. It doesn't take a fancy production type of video to make money. Some of the most profitable videos are simple 3-minute videos demonstrating Disney toys. If you want to get an idea of what topics get a lot of YouTube views, you can see the top 100 moneymakers on YouTube at the link below:

SocialBlade.com/youtube/top/country/US

4. **Sell items on Amazon or eBay.** Buy closeout items from Walmart or buy items from China (through Alibaba.com) and sell them on Amazon or eBay.

5. **Use your computer to do freelance creative work.** There are four major websites that help you get jobs (or gigs as they are called) to do this kind of work.

   • Elance.com

   • Odesk.com

   • Freelancer.com

   • Fiverr.com

The website that I have used the most is Fiverr.com. There are hundreds of categories of services you can provide. You could do proofreading, design logos, design book covers, etc. In fact, I hired people from Fiverr to design the cover of this book, and I also hired a proofreader to read the book. Go to Fiverr.com and check them out. While you're at the website, go through the steps and become a gig provider in one or more categories and give it a try.

I won't try to cover all of the details about how to make money using Fiverr in this book. A whole book could be written about the topic. In fact, I just did a search on Amazon and found that 261 books have been written about how to make money using Fiverr.

One of the highest rated ones is *The Fiverr Masters Class.* The eBook is only $3.99 and you can find it by searching Amazon for the title of the book.

You don't have to select just one of the money-making techniques described above. I have several income streams. One word of caution; don't fall for any of the work-at-home scams that you see on the internet. Don't get involved with any scheme that requires you to pay money upfront.

**Bottom line:** You can live on a boat cheaper than you can live in a traditional house, apartment or condo, so if you want to be a liveaboard, read the rest of this book, check out the additional information referred to in the *Other Resources* chapter, and then start taking steps to make it happen.

As this chapter pointed out, being a liveaboard and living on a typical Social Security check is quite possible and following the techniques described to make a little extra money will allow you to really enjoy a retirement of fun, adventure, and relaxation.

# Chapter 15:

---

# Ways Boaters Stretch Their Money

---

*"It's nice to get out of the rat race, but you have to learn to get along with less cheese."*

~ Gene Perret

The liveaboard lifestyle is (or maybe I should say it can be) much less expensive than living the conventional lifestyle. One important thing you have to remember is that moving onto a boat won't automatically change who you are (or how you spend money). You have to make a conscious decision to change your habits.

Many boaters tell me that they spent a lot more money the first year they were living on their boats than they do now. A lot of new liveaboards spend too much money adding gadgets to their boats that are nice but not necessary.

The purpose of this chapter is to teach you how to immediately implement the techniques that it took many liveaboards a year or more to learn—that is how to enjoy wine and roses on a water and daisy budget.

## The 11 Common Ways Liveaboards Stretch Their Dollars

1. **Going shopping is no longer a form of entertainment.** You only go shopping when you really need something and even then consider buying what you need from Amazon. You can usually get a better price, and you're not tempted to buy other stuff like you would on a shopping trip.

2. **Buy clothes from Goodwill and thrift shops.** I bought two shirts from Goodwill recently for $4 each. One was an L.L. Bean shirt and one was a Lands End shirt. Both of these shirts retail for over $50. If you listen to the conversations at happy hour gatherings, you'll soon learn that a lot of full-time liveaboards shop for some of their clothes at Goodwill.

3. **You're not on a permanent vacation.** You can't take in all of the tourist attractions, eat out all the time

and stay on your budget. Enjoying happy hours on the dock with fellow liveaboards instead of going to the local watering holes all the time is a popular form of entertainment for liveaboards.

4. **When you want to go out to eat, search out little mom and pop restaurants.** The big, fancy restaurants where all of the tourists go are usually overpriced, and I find that most of them are not unique. They're just cookie-cutter tourist restaurants. Fellow liveaboards will tell you where the nearby, small hole-in-the-wall restaurants are that serve great local food at non-tourist prices. Tourist restaurants don't give you a flavor of the local area anyway. And, of course, don't go out to eat very often. Going out to eat should be a special event. Treat it that way and you will enjoy the experience a lot more.

5. **Don't waste food by putting leftovers in the refrigerator for a few days and then tossing them out.** Food is one of the biggest things in your budget so, naturally, it presents one of the biggest opportunities to save money. One of the best ways to save money is not to waste food by throwing it out. Plan most meals by looking at the leftovers that are in the refrigerator and then deciding what you will need to go with those leftovers to make a meal. If you don't want the same thing two meals in a row,

at least plan to use the leftovers at the following meal. By all means, don't just put leftovers in the back of the refrigerator and forget about them for a few days. After all, liveaboard refrigerators are small, and it doesn't take many half-empty bowls to take up all of the room. Look at it this way, the more leftovers you eat the more money there will be in the budget to go out to eat.

6. **Make it a habit to check eBay and Craigslist before you buy almost anything.** Buying used (and sometimes new) items through eBay and Craigslist can easily save you 50% or more on most items. I buy items on Amazon too, but I usually find new items on Amazon and used items on eBay and Craigslist. I bought a used Progressive Industries portable electrical management system (a little box to protect against electrical surges, open ground wires, low voltage, etc.) through eBay for about half of the retail price.

7. **Check out garage sales.** In addition to finding real bargains, going to garage sales is a great way to get to see the local area.

8. Another way to save money big-time is to **realize that things don't make you happy.** Think about all of the stuff that you will have to get rid of if you switch to the liveaboard lifestyle. Think about all of

the items you have bought that you don't use. When you're considering a purchase (whether it's an expensive item or a relatively inexpensive one), stop and think about whether you will really use it all that much and whether you will actually be happier a week or a month from now because you have it.

9. **Learning to be content with what you have** is one of the best ways in the world to save money—and it's a lot easier to do when you're living the liveaboard lifestyle. Liveaboards are not much into keeping up with the Joneses. Of course, there are big, fancy boats, but, for the most part, liveaboards consider boats as they would pets. They don't even think about who has an expensive boat and who has a cheap one any more than they think about who has an expensive dog and who has a rescue dog. Everyone's boat is and dog is special, and they love them both.

10. **Live on the hook or at a mooring ball part of the time**. It's a great way to save money and many liveaboards take advantage of it from time to time. Of course, be careful and don't give up your marina slip if there is a waiting list. Living on the hook or tied to a mooring ball is a good choice for the last month or two before you leave to go to another marina. A lot of liveaboards like to move with the

seasons or, at least, move to a different marina every year or so just for a change of scenery.

11.**Do some of your own boat maintenance**. Instead of paying a boat service center $125 an hour or more, consider learning how to do some of the work yourself. You can get a mobile boat technician to come out and spend a few hours with you and show you where a lot of things are and how to repair a lot of routine items. Having this knowledge will save you a lot of money in the long run. The more you know about your boat, the less money it will cost you to maintain it.

Don't get me wrong; you can't do all of the maintenance on your boat. For some things you will need the mechanic at the marina to do the work. After all, you can't haul your boat out of the water by yourself.

**One last point:** There's a difference between being frugal and being cheap. Being frugal means that you show good judgment in the way you choose to spend your money. It's a mark of status today. It used to be that people kept it a secret when they bought something at Goodwill; now they brag about it.

**Bottom line:** By themselves, none of the techniques I've described in this chapter will work wonders with your budget, but when you use all of them on a consistent basis, the savings will add up.

---

# Chapter 16

# How to Get Rid of Your Stuff

---

*"A house is just a place to keep your stuff while you go out and get more stuff."*

~ George Carlin

You *can* take it with you—but you can't take all of it.

I don't know how many times I've heard someone say, "I could never live on a boat—I have too much stuff." If this describes your thinking, remember the stuff doesn't own you. You own the stuff.

People say this with so much conviction, just as they would say that one leg is longer than the other one.

They act like they were born that way and that there is nothing they can do about it.

If you say, "I choose to have all of this stuff," then you own the situation or problem. It's easier to deal with when you look at it that way.

Your stuff can all be classified into one of four categories, A, B, C and D:

**Category A:** Things you really are going to use and take with you on your boat—and remember a boat can hold more stuff if you know how to pack every little space.

**Category B:** These are the things that you can sell— your dining room table and chairs, the sofa you bought two years ago, your riding lawnmower. In fact, you can sell almost everything and it doesn't take long to do it.

CraigsList is a great way to sell larger items. If you price the items right and include pictures, they will usually sell within a week. If an item doesn't sell within a week, lower the price by at least a third and list it again. Be sure to list a phone number where you can be reached most of the time.

When someone is ready to buy something, if they can't get you on the phone, they will call another person selling essentially the same type of item you're offering. I have sold a lot of items using CraigsList. The system works great. You get a fair price and you get it sold quickly.

For smaller items, you can use eBay. For both CraigsList and eBay, be sure to show several good quality pictures. Pictures help items sell quickly. With eBay, you can set a reserve price or you can just auction it off and take what you get. After all, usually, whatever it sells for is what it's worth and that's what you wanted to do in the first place—sell the item for whatever it's worth.

I like to run an eBay auction for three days and start the bidding at $1. That gets a lot of people bidding. You can also offer a "Buy It Now" option with eBay. A lot of people don't want to wait. They want to buy your item and be done with it.

**Category C:** These are the things that you put in a garage sale one Saturday and then take what doesn't sell to Goodwill. This way, at the end of the day, everything in this category is gone.

Basically, Category C items are things that you could buy at Goodwill for almost nothing *IF* you ever really needed them. In this category would be tools you won't need, old furniture, clothes, shoes, items you bought at garage sales because they were such bargains, all the extra dishes and cookware that won't fit in your boat, all of the extra towels and linens. The list goes on. But get rid of these things in a hurry.

**Category D:** This category is for sentimental things. A few of these things you may want to put in storage but very few. Pictures and photo albums can all be scanned and put on a thumb drive. If you don't know how to do this, there are businesses that offer this service at a very low price.

There's Grandma's sewing machine, Great Grandma's lamp, the afghan that Aunt Sarah made for you, etc. Most people think that things on this list are the hardest to get rid of. But in fact, these items can be the easiest to get rid of if you follow the procedure described below.

First of all, decide who you want to have each of these things when you're dead and gone. (I know you consider that to be a long way off, but think about it this way anyway.) Then give the items to them now. If they won't take the things now, you know what will happen to them as soon as you're gone. They will give them to Goodwill, sell them in a garage sale or just throw them away. If you have a few items that you want your grandchildren to have when they're grown, you can put these items in storage if you can't convince their parents to keep the items for them.

I know that it's hard to accept the fact that a lot of things you cherish will not even be considered worth keeping by other people when you're gone. That's just a fact. Don't blame your relatives. It's not their responsibility or duty to like or value the same things you like.

Remember when you give someone something, it's theirs. Be sure to tell them this. If they want to sell it in a garage sale, that's fine with you. Of course, that's probably not the way you feel, but there's no need to lay a guilt trip on them and insist that they keep the item and cherish it. Even if they do keep it for a while, it may get thrown away later.

A lot of the things you will be giving people will be things that they will love and really enjoy having. By giving them the items now, you'll get to see them enjoy the things and you'll know the items went to the people you wanted to have them.

By all means don't just put things in storage—at least, not more than what will fit in the smallest storage unit they make.

If you do put things in a storage unit, consider getting rid of even those things a year from now. Some people have found it easier to get rid of sentimental things in a two-step process like this, but don't let it drag out for years and still have your belongings in storage.

In other words, put those things you think you just can't part with in storage for one year. At the end of a year, decide if your future is full-time living aboard your boat. If so, give everything that's in storage that you're not actually going to use to your relatives. If they don't want it, sell it. If it doesn't sell, give it to Goodwill or throw it away.

I know of one couple who put things in a storage unit and didn't even see any of the things for seven years before they finally decided to go back and empty out the storage unit. The items in their storage unit were not sentimental things, just stuff.

I also know a woman who has a very large storage unit that she pays $200 a month for and she has had it for over 5 years. That's over $12,000 she has paid and I wouldn't give $200 for everything in her storage unit. Most of it's not even sentimental items; it's just things she thinks she might need someday. Don't fall into this trap. Even $50 a month for five years is still $3,000 and $3,000 will buy a lot of stuff.

Look at it this way, if you put a big, new storage building behind your house, how long do you think it would be before it would be full? We all tend to store stuff until all available space is filled.

It will feel like a tremendous burden is lifted from your shoulders when you have gotten rid of all of the stuff you don't really need.

One thing that helps in getting rid of things is to set a date by which everything has to be gone. For a storage unit that can be easy, just say, "I'm not going to pay another month's rent. Everything has to be out by the last day of the month."

## There Is Some Wiggle Room

Now that I've convinced you to get rid of most of your stuff and shown you how to do it, let me back up and tell you that you do have a little bit of wiggle room. Many boaters get a small storage unit (as close by as possible) and they keep a few tools and other things that they need and use in this storage unit.

This is not for storing things you don't want to get rid of. It's mainly for keeping extra tools, spare parts, winter or summer clothes and things that you will actually use from time to time.

If you need extra help getting rid of stuff, I have written a book, *Tidying Up,* that you might find helpful. Here is a link to it on Amazon:

https://www.amazon.com/dp/0984496882

# Tidying Up

THE MAGIC AND SECRETS OF
DECLUTTERING
YOUR HOME AND YOUR LIFE

JERRY MINCHEY

**Bottom line:** You have all of this stuff because you choose to have it. Therefore, you can choose to get rid of it. You may not believe it now but it's such a big relief when you get rid of all of the stuff that you've been hanging on to for years.

I know one couple who made a picture of their empty storage unit and then threw a party and invited their friends to help them celebrate the big occasion. It was a fun time.

Plan your party now to celebrate your freedom from STUFF!

---

# Chapter 17

# Choosing a Marina

---

*"Most people who died yesterday had plans for today.*
*Don't take life for granted."*

~ Unknown

Once you own a boat one of the main things to consider is where you're going to park it. If you're going to be cruising, it's not a problem. You won't be parking it at all—except for occasionally docking at an interesting place to do some exploring or docking to get more supplies.

You could live "on the hook", which means you are tied to a hook (an anchor) instead of being tied to a dock at a marina.

The best part about living on the hook is that you're floating for free in a cove, up a river or out in the open water. This is a viable option with advantages and disadvantages. Several members of our group have lived on the hook for a year or more at a time. They said that they would come to shore every now and then for supplies and to socialize with friends. I covered the option of living on the hook in detail back in chapter 7.

For most liveaboards, where to park comes down to selecting a marina. Your ideal marina will depend on a lot of factors. Do you want a secluded place with no interruptions so you can finish writing a book (or work on other projects)? Do you want a place where there are a lot of social activities and where you can stagger (I mean walk) back to your boat from the bars? Do you want a place that is close to your day job?

Selecting a marina is like selecting a neighborhood. Whether you will like the liveaboard lifestyle or not will have a lot to do with how well you like the marina you choose. Some boaters stay in one marina all the time and some move around every few months (or years). Most of the people in our discussion group said that they liked to move around to different marinas.

I would highly recommend that you have a firm commitment to a place to park your boat before you buy it. Don't assume that you can just go to the marina you like and rent a slip. Hopefully, you can, but that's not always the case.

Some marinas have waiting lists (sometimes for years); some only allow a certain number of liveaboards; some don't allow certain kinds of boats (such as old boats). Also, make sure that you and the marina agree on the length of your boat. Since most slips are charged for based on the length of your boat, how they determine the length of your boat can make a big difference in the price you will be paying for your slip. Keep in mind that sometimes this is negotiable.

One other thing to keep in mind is that, just because the boat you're buying is in a slip, you shouldn't assume that you can take over paying the rent and keep it there. Maybe you can, and maybe you can't, but do your homework and don't take it for granted.

Here are the features that the members of our group agreed were important to them when selecting a marina.

## Ten Things to Consider When Selecting a Marina

1. **Clean bathrooms and showers.** Here's how one woman explained her thoughts on bathrooms at marinas: "I like having a convenient and clean bath house. The showers are larger than what's on my boat and by using their shower, I don't have to pump out my holding tanks as often and it helps keep the humidity down in the boat. Also, I get to take long showers when I'm using their hot water."

2. **Well maintained laundry facilities.** Most marinas have laundry facilities but some of them are not well maintained. Here are one liveaboard's comments: "I was at one marina that had three washers and dryers and only one washer was working. I was at one where no one serviced the machines on the weekends, and when the coin containers filled up, the machines would not accept any more quarters and, of course, then they wouldn't work. This happened a lot. You can't tell this by looking at the machines, so ask other liveaboards about how reliable the laundry facilities are."

3. **Easy access to the rest of the world.** It's nice to be able to walk to restaurants, watering holes, and shops (or at least ride a bicycle). One member of the group said, "I was at one marina where I had to

drive 30 miles to get to town. That was nice for a while, because I wanted to 'get away from it all', but it soon got old." If you're going to work every day, staying in a marina that's convenient to your work is a big plus. If you want to do a lot of sailing, select a marina that has easy access to open water. Another member of the group chimed in and said, "I've stayed at marinas where it took me 30 minutes to an hour to get out to the open waters. Of course, it wasn't all bad. These marinas were much lower cost than the ones with easy access to open water."

4. **A staffed office where you can receive mail and packages.** This can also serve as your official address. If you like to move around from time to time, you could use a mail forwarding service for your official address on your driver's license, etc. That way you don't have to change things every time you move. You can still order items from Amazon or eBay and have them shipped to your marina address. I guess you could say that you would have two addresses—a permanent address and a temporary address.

5. **High-speed and strong WiFi signal.** This is an important consideration for most people. Some marinas have a stronger WiFi signal at some slips than at others, so be sure to check out how strong

the WiFi signal is at the actual slip you will be occupying. If you do much work on the internet, be sure to do an internet speed test. Just because there is a strong signal, it doesn't mean that you will have a fast internet connection. You can run an internet speed test at http://www.speedtest.net

You can always get a Verizon Jetpack or other hotspot devices from other carriers to get a fast internet connection, but that will cost you $100 or so a month and if you can get by with the marina WiFi connection, that will save you some money. By the way, as of March, 2017 most of the wireless internet providers have started providing unlimited wireless data plans, but read the fine print. They're not really unlimited. All of the providers are changing their plans almost weekly, so check them all out to find the best deal you can get if you decide to go with one of the wireless carriers.

6. **Well designed and well maintained.** I think everyone in the group agreed that they didn't want to pay an arm and a leg for a resort type atmosphere, but they did like the docks to be reasonably clean, have adequate lighting, and have trash cans that were emptied frequently. I guess you get what you pay for, but they all agreed that they didn't want to live in a place that looked trashy.

7. **Price.** The monthly fee that marinas charge is important, but you can't just compare the prices because you have to check to see what is included in the price. Sometimes electricity is included and sometimes it's extra. The same goes for cable TV. A lot of liveaboards who are on a budget just use an antenna and only watch the TV stations that they can pick up with their antenna. Also, some marinas charge more for liveaboards, and some charge more if you have an air conditioner. Almost all marinas charge by the foot, but some of them get creative about how they determine the length of your boat. When checking the price, make sure you have a firm price quote for your particular boat and the way you will be using it.

8. **Storage.** Are there storage units nearby and how much do they cost?

9. **Parking.** How convenient and secure is the parking area? Is it well lit? How much does a parking space cost? Is free parking included in the price you're paying for the slip rental? Is there adequate parking for guests?

10. **Well protected.** Wakes and waves caused by the wind or passing boats can wreak havoc with your life as a liveaboard. Selecting a marina that doesn't slam you against the walls or knock you out of bed

at night is one of the most important things most liveaboards consider when choosing a marina. Noises you can usually get used to, but excessive rocking is one thing that most liveaboards consider to be a deal killer. In fact, everyone agreed that excessive rocking should be the first thing on the list of deal killers when selecting a marina. Here is the list:

## Deal Killers

There are some things to look out for that could be considered "deal killers". One big thing to look out for is how protected the marina is. If there are big wakes caused by other boats or by winds that can rock you and your boat that would be a deal killer for a lot of people. Some people can tolerate it. Some said that they could tolerate it when they were out cruising and the water was rough, but it's not something they wanted to be subjected to on a constant basis.

It's always nice to have a low monthly rental fee, but you usually get about what you pay for. One member of our group made these comments: "I remember visiting one marina with fairly low fees, but when I checked them out, I found that there were a lot of unemployed people on trashy boats living there. The bathhouse wasn't clean, and there was trash everywhere. I didn't even bother to ask if they had slips available. I decided that this marina wouldn't be for me even if it were free."

Another person said, "If I see drug use or drug dealing going on, that's a deal killer for me. It may be going on at almost all marinas, but if it's out in the open, and they are not even trying to hide it, I sure don't want to be around that behavior. Also, my thinking is that if someone is using a lot of drugs, they would likely steal me blind."

I'm sure you may have other things that are deal killers for you. Be sure to check things out thoroughly, and know what you're getting into. It's a good idea to visit a prospective marina in the mornings, in the early evenings and again in the later evenings to get a good feel for what's going on and what it would be like living in that neighborhood.

## Nice Extra Features to Have

In addition to deal killers, sometimes there are some features that are nice to have, but not necessary, such as: mobile pump-out service, fire-pit area for cook-outs, jam sessions, socializing, easy access to open water, easy access to public transportation, group gatherings hosted by the marina, etc.

**Bottom line:** Decide what features are important to you—which ones are "must-haves" and which ones are deal killers. Be sure to talk to several liveaboards at the marina, get a feel for whether liveaboards are really welcome or just tolerated. Check out the items listed previously and spend time looking around.

Do all of this and then you can make your selection. Go with your gut feel. It's almost like picking out roommates. In a lot of marinas boats are so close together that in a way they are all roommates.

Of course, there may be situations where for the time being you don't have much choice. For example, there may be only one marina that's close enough to your work to be feasible, but go with the flow and realize that things change.

# Chapter 18:

---

# Emotional Aspects of the Liveaboard Lifestyle

---

*"Nobody can go back and start a new beginning, but anyone can start today and make a new ending."*
~ Maria Robinson


You can look at the numbers until you're blue in the face. On paper, everything looks like it will work out great, but you still have that uneasy feeling in your gut. Questions keep popping into your head such as, *Will I be happy? Will it work? What if?*

Taking the plunge to become a liveaboard is a major life-changing event. All liveaboards have these feelings and a flood of emotions when they're contemplating taking the leap. The feelings are normal, but you have to deal with them and the best way to deal with them is to be prepared for them and be expecting them.

When you announce your plans to your family and friends, they will throw up even more questions, doubts and fears for you to consider.

There will be doubts and questions all along the way—when you announce your plans while you're preparing to make the transition, and even after you get your boat and move on board.

## Here Are Some of the Questions That May Haunt You from Time to Time

- Am I being realistic?
- Will this really work?
- Will my family and friends think I'm crazy?
- Will I be lonely?
- Is this a mistake?

When you hear these questions in your head, think of what some wise people have had to say about life, as stated in their quotes below:

*"Whenever you find yourself on the side of the majority, it's time to pause and reflect."*

~ Mark Twain

*"When in doubt, choose change."*

~ Lily Leung

*"Your life does not get better by chance, it gets better by change."*

~ Jim Rohn

And the quote I like best is. . .

*"If you come to a fork in the road, take it."*

~ Yogi Berra

When you're living the liveaboard lifestyle, you will be free to follow Yogi's advice.

Reflecting on some of these famous quotes will help convince you that you're making the right decision. After all, you've already gone through the numbers, and you know from a logical standpoint that you're making the right decision.

## The Emotional Part of Becoming a Liveaboard Comes Down to Five Areas:

### 1. Selling your home or moving out of your apartment

Downsizing from a stick-and-brick home can be scary and overwhelming. What if you change your mind? Maybe you could keep your house and rent it out. If you need the equity in your house to buy your boat, it's a simple decision—you either sell it or you stay put. It's not an easy decision, but it is a simple one.

If you're leaving an apartment that you're renting, it's a lot less stressful. This is a personal matter, but you must go through the numbers, make the decision and then live with your emotions. Most people tell me it was a very liberating feeling when their house was sold and they became free to enjoy the liveaboard lifestyle.

One other thing to think about is that you're probably ready for a change or you wouldn't even be considering the liveaboard lifestyle. And even if you later decide you don't like living on a boat, you probably don't want to go back to your previous life or to the exact same house or apartment that you're unhappy with now.

## 2. Getting rid of your stuff

The logistics of how to get rid of your stuff were covered in chapter 16. I talked about the techniques that would make the process easy, but I didn't talk about the emotions involved in the process. This is the one area that gives people a lot of worries and has them asking, "What if?"

The truth of the matter is I have never talked to anyone who said they missed all of that stuff. In fact, I don't remember anyone ever saying that they miss a single item. It's such a load off of them when all of that stuff is gone. You could put all of your stuff in storage, but that gets expensive. If you feel that you have to put everything in storage, it probably means you're not ready to simplify your life.

If you're having trouble getting rid of your stuff, go back and re-read chapter 16 and follow the simple steps I have outlined. That's how I got rid of my stuff, and the technique worked (quickly and easily).

## 3. How to deal with your family's reactions when you announce your plans

Some might think you've lost your mind (others will probably be sure). Some will be envious and some will think it's a phase that you will soon grow out of and that you will soon come back to your senses.

When you announce your plans to your family and friends, be prepared to answer some questions and show them that you've thought things out and have a clear plan.

### 4. Dealing with being away from family and friends

If you're going to be living at a marina near to where you're living now, you won't be away from your family and friends. But if you're going to be cruising or living at a marina that's not near where you're living now, you will have to deal with being away from them.

This turns out to be not nearly as difficult as most people expect it to be. With email, Skype and cell phones, you can stay in touch as much as you want to—there just won't be as much face time. You will stay in touch with a few friends but not as many as you think, mainly because you won't have as much in common with them as you do now.

You will find that you will be spending a lot more time with your new liveaboard friends because you will have so much more in common with them. I've heard several liveaboards say that they have a lot more friends since they embarked on the liveaboard lifestyle than they ever had when they lived in a house or apartment.

## 5. Feelings to expect after you move onto your boat

You'll be questioning yourself for a while after you start living on your boat. This is normal. The future is unknown but, realistically, it's unknown in your present lifestyle too.

Accept the fact that the emotions and doubts you feel when you first start out are normal. They will fade quickly when the excitement kicks in. How can you feel down when every day is a new adventure?

From time to time, if you need to go through all of the reasons you wanted to live the liveaboard lifestyle and go over all of the numbers again that you crunched to make sure it would work, it's fine to do it, but at some point you have to accept the fact that here you are. Enjoy the journey.

You always have the option to go back to your previous life, but give it a year. My bet is that going back will not happen—at least, not anytime soon.

## The Next Phase—The Emotional Part of Living Aboard a Boat

In addition to the emotions you will experience while you're getting ready to move onto your boat, there will be emotions to deal with once you're living there too.

Knowing what to expect and being prepared for the emotional parts of the liveaboard life will help you handle (and enjoy) this lifestyle.

Face the fact that there will be a huge emotional challenge when you leave your home. Leaving your home (and maybe you'll be changing jobs or retiring), and maybe leaving family and friends all at once can be a big blow. Yes, it can be downright scary. Accept this feeling as normal.

Instead of making one big leap, some people think about putting their stuff in storage and renting out their house for a year so they can come back to it if they change their minds. My thoughts are that if you think you're ready for a change, you probably are. You may find that the liveaboard lifestyle is not the change you want, but I'm betting that going back to the life you left is not it either.

If you decide the liveaboard life is not the life for you, you will be ready to move on to something else—a different town, a different house or apartment, a different job, maybe even living in a different country. (I lived for six months in Costa Rica and thoroughly enjoyed it.) Whatever you decide to do, I'm betting that living the conventional lifestyle in the proverbial rat race is not how you want to live.

## Meeting New Friends

As many liveaboards have told me, they have a lot more friends now that they're living full time on their boats. You'll find that since all liveaboards are away from their previous neighborhoods, they are all looking to meet new friends.

You will be welcome at happy hours and around the campfire (many marinas have a place for a campfire), and it doesn't matter what size boat you have.

**Bottom line:** Yes, you will have to deal with a lot of emotions when it comes to embarking on the liveaboard lifestyle. Consider your emotions and let them guide you to go over and over your plans and decisions, but if the numbers say you can do it, and it's what you want to do, don't let fear of the unknown keep you from embarking on your dream.

Consider this advice from Steve Jobs. . .

*"Don't let the noise of others' opinions drown out your own inner voice. And most important, have the courage to follow your heart and intuition."*

~ Steve Jobs

# Chapter 19:

---

# Living Aboard Solo

---

Live your life so you can say,

> *"When I grow up, I want to be like me."*
>
> ~ Unknown

Teresa Carey bought her 27-foot Nor'Sea sailboat named Daphne and became a liveaboard solo sailor back in 2008.

You might wonder how a female as small as she is can sail a 27-foot boat all by herself. Her answer is simple and straight to the point. She said,

"You don't need large muscles to sail a boat solo; you need a large spirit."

You can follow her on her blog at http://sailingsimplicity.com and, if you want her to teach you to sail, at certain times of the year she takes four or five students at a time for a 10-day training course with hands-on sailing from Florida to the Bahamas. She offers other programs too. That's one of the ways she makes her living while living the liveaboard lifestyle.

Spend a lot of time on Teresa's website. It has more useful sailing articles and information than any website I know of. I highly recommend it.

Update: Teresa is married now and is no longer sailing solo, but she's still sailing and being more adventuresome than ever. Many of the older articles on her website are about her time as a solo sailor.

## Another Solo Sailor

Not long ago, 29-year-old Emily Richardson left California and sailed south. She's on a journey around the world with no schedule in mind. She has an old boat. She says that she sails to the next port, fixes what's broken, sails to the next port and fixes what's broken and on she goes. She is presently in the Indian Ocean and plans to sail to Sri Lanka next and then on to East Africa on her journey around the world. Of course, by the time you read this, there's no telling where she will be.

Here is a picture of the inside of her boat. It looks organized, cozy, and functional.

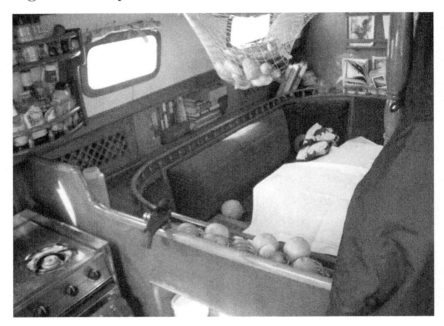

*Inside Emily's boat. (Photo courtesy of Cameron Smith)*

Here's a link to Cameron Smith's interview with her where she talks about her journey around the world:

http://indefinitelywild.gizmodo.com/meet-the-29-year-old-girl-sailing-around-the-world-sol-1613592153

(By the way, this article first appeared on

www.Gizmodo.com. Check it out for other interesting articles on topics other than sailing.)

## These two stories are typical of what magazines and newspapers like to write about

People like to dream, and writers like to help them dream. Cruising around the world is the dream of many liveaboard sailors, but the truth of the matter is that most liveaboards never leave the marina and the ones who do only do so for short excursions.

Part of the charm and intrigue of being a liveaboard is not so much that you're going to take off and sail around the world or sail around in the Caribbean but that you know you can do it (with a little preparation) anytime you really want to. Having the freedom and ability to do it when and if you want to is enough for most liveaboards.

As one member of our group said, "I have lived solo on different boats—from a 44-foot houseboat to my present boat, a 20-feet Nimble20 sailboat. It's an interesting life. I never know what I'll encounter or who I'll meet or how long I'll stay in one place. Right now my boat is out of the water being worked on and I'm staying with a friend.

"One of the things I like about being a solo liveaboard is that I can change my mind and plans at any time. The decisions are mine to make, and the consequences are mine to bear."

## Security

One of the major concerns for many people who are considering becoming a liveaboard, especially women, is security, which is a valid concern but not one that should keep you from making the decision. The next chapter is all about safety and security, so I won't go into it in detail here, except to say that, with a little common sense and reasonable precautions, you're probably safer on a boat than you are living in a house or condo.

## Loneliness

If you're cruising or out living on the hook, you could get lonely, but if you're living at the marina, there are probably more things going on and more camaraderie than where you're living now.

One member of the group described loneliness this way: "When I'm living on the hook or cruising, I enjoy the solitude and the time by myself. Knowing that I can go to the marina or into a port anytime I want to gives me the freedom to have exactly the mixture I want of time by myself and time with other people. I like being in control of my social life."

Whether you consider yourself to be an introvert or an extrovert will have a lot to do with whether you want a lot of time by yourself or a lot of time being around people. We all need some of both, and we change some from time to time. We are not always completely one way or the other.

Here's one good way to prevent loneliness and isolation. Stay in contact with the people you already know and care about—at least the ones you want to keep a close relationship with. With email, cell phones, Skype, and a little effort, it can be done. I'm sure you would like it better if they would take the initiative and call or email you, but if they don't, there's nothing keeping you from calling or emailing them.

Some of your previous relationships will not survive. They were based on factors that have changed. What did you have in common with these people—work, church, hobbies, they were neighbors, etc.? Whatever connection drew you together may no longer exist and the relationship will fade in time. That's not all bad.

Some of your old relationships will survive. It's not like you dropped off the face of the earth. You will still see them from time to time. You may find that you'll be staying in touch more when you're living on a boat than you did before. It's just that you don't have as much face time. You will be replacing these friends with new friends who share common interests with you.

One member of the group put it this way: "I like to have time to work on my projects with no interruptions. I'm a lot more productive that way. I work as long or as late as I want to, and I take a nap when I want to. I'm usually up and doing things by 7:00 a.m., often working on a project (writing, doing research, etc.). Whatever I do, I like to start early (with a cup of tea green, of course)."

Liveaboards are by nature a very friendly bunch, but they also respect your privacy.

If you have a dog, you can soon meet everyone in the marina while you're walking him.

## Four Other Things for a Solo Liveaboard to Consider

After you've conquered security and loneliness there's not much more to be concerned about as a solo liveaboard, but if you really need a few other things to think about, here are seven things you should do or at least consider—and, by the way, these things are important for all liveaboards, but they are especially important if you're living solo.

1. **Get active on boating forums:** There are lots of boating forums and most of them have their discussions broken down into topics. The advantages of reading and participating in forums is that you will learn a lot from reading answers to other people's questions, you can get your own questions answered, and you can make a lot of friends.

   Here is a link to my favorite boating forum:

   **http://sailnet.com**

   Just click on the word "Forums" in the top nav. bar and then you can select from forums on several different topics. Spend a lot of time reading the questions and answers on the different forums. It's a great way to learn and you'll quickly get to know a lot of boating terms. For example, if you say something about the miles per hour of your boat instead of using the word "knots", people will know you're a novice boater. No problem. They'll still be friendly and answer your question. Don't be afraid to jump in and ask questions.

2. **Make copies of all of your important documents:** For peace of mind it's a good idea to make copies of all of your credit cards (both sides), your driver's

license, passport, Social Security card, and birth certificate. Keep a copy hidden in your boat and leave another copy with a friend or relative.

3. **Read your boating manual and learn as much about your boat as you can:** This is particularly important if you plan do any cruising. I agree that most boat manuals leave a lot to be desired, but spend time finding out what information is included. Learn as much as you can about your boat. When you buy it and someone is going over everything with you (and they will), be sure to video the demonstration. If you're buying it from an individual, write his name, phone number, and email address down and keep it with your boat manual and other information. More than likely, there will be a time when you would like to call him and ask questions.

The more you know about your boat the more secure and in control you will feel. Know what all of the gauges and electronic readouts and lights mean. If you're a female, don't fall into the old-school thinking that you can't do certain things.

Also, keep all service and repair documentation. This will be helpful to you and it will increase the resale value when you can show a prospective buyer all that has been done and that routine maintenance has been performed on a regular basis.

4. **Get a marine GPS (and know how to use it) if you plan to do any cruising (plus have a set of charts):** A GPS is handy to have, but make sure you fully know how to use it and can take advantage of all its features.

**Bottom line:** I'm amazed at how many solo boaters there are. I'm convinced that living solo on a boat is safer than living in a conventional home. And I know it's more fun, so don't let the fact that you will be a solo liveaboard be a reason not to enjoy the liveaboard lifestyle.

## Chapter 20:

---

# Safety and Security

---

*"Being on a boat that's moving through the water, it's so clear. Everything falls into place in terms of what's important and what's not."*

~ James Taylor

Most of this chapter was written by one of the most experienced and safety conscious liveaboards I know. In keeping with the format of the rest of this book, he said, "Don't bother with my name. Just use my knowledge, information and experience in a way that will help keep everyone reading this." He went on to say, "I don't want credit. I just want everyone to be safe." Here's what he had to say:

"When I think of safety, I think of accidents and the actions I can take to prevent them and protect myself, my guests, and my crew (when I'm lucky enough to have a crew).

"When I think about security, ideas about bad people stealing things (even the boat), destroying things or doing harm to me come to mind."

In this chapter I'll discuss safety and security with those basic definitions in mind.

## Safety

Some of the basic safety equipment is required by law, but there are other pieces of equipment that I like to have that are not actually required, but it makes good sense to have the extra items on board.

## Here is a List of the Safety Equipment I Recommend:

### Five Coast Guard Required Safety Items

1.  Life jackets (for every person on board)
2.  Sound signaling device, (horn, whistle, or bell)

3. Fire extinguisher (one is required. I have two)

4. Throwable floatation item (such as an approved floatation cushion)

5. Visual distress signal

One other thing that I highly recommend is to have a Coast Guard approved VHF marine radio. In fact, I like to have two VHF radios—one is installed in the cabin and I carry a backup handheld radio. Don't depend on your cell phone. If you get very far off shore, you probably won't have a reliable signal.

I also like to have a marine GPS. They're handy even if you only venture out of the marina occasionally. You can get them from under $200 to well over $1,000. Analyze the different features, your needs, and your budget and select the one that's best for you. Of course, you can get by without one (or maybe one will come with the boat when you buy it). I went for years without one, but they sure are nice.

In addition to equipment, here are some other things you should do that will go a long way towards preventing accidents.

• Know your boat.

• Know the navigation rules.

• Have an anchor on board.

- Take a boating safety course.

- Sail with other boat captains from time to time and learn from them.

Below are links to two websites that have a lot of useful safety information:

http://www.usps.org/index.html

http://powerboat.about.com/od/safetyandeducation/tp/Boating-Best-Practices.htm

## Children and Safety

If you have children on board, you need to take a lot of special precautions. Boats cannot be made as safe as a house for children, but there are a lot of things you can and should do to make it as safe as possible. The most important thing is to keep the kids from falling overboard. And since they likely will fall overboard at some time or another, make sure they wear life jackets when they're on the deck—no exceptions. There are inflatable life jackets that are not as restrictive as conventional ones.

While cruising, I like the idea of children wearing a harness because things happen fast and you can't always keep an eye on them. With wind, a slick deck, and the boat heeled over at a steep angle, there's a really good chance that, if you have children on board, one of them is going to fall overboard sooner or later.

It's not just being on the boat that's inherently dangerous. Docks can be slick and there are lots of things for a child to trip on when they're on the dock. Children have lots of energy and the first thing they want to do when they get off of the boat is start running. Running while on a dock can be dangerous. Have a rule (and enforce it) of no running on the dock. Of course, by all means, as soon as you get the kids to a safe place, let them run their legs off. They need the exercise.

Also, keep in mind that there are a lot of dangerous things on a boat and there are ways for a child to get hurt even when the boat is tied at the dock. There are lines, switches, knobs, gas burners, steps, and the list goes on and on. All of these things are within easy reach or stick out and get in the way—particularly when kids are not paying attention.

Your children will soon learn about all of the dangers and be careful, but you have to be especially careful when children are visiting. Everything is new to them. They will be exploring, playing, and in general not paying a lot of attention to being safe. They're not used to having to be careful, so it's your job to look after them.

Of course, most of the dangers and things to be aware of described above apply to adults (including you) as well.

Training and strict adherence to safety rules and procedures are important. It's your job as captain of the ship to make sure that you, your crew, your family, and your guests follow all of the safety rules and procedures. This is especially important when people are sitting around having a beer or a glass of wine.

Sitting on the deck with a glass of wine and watching the sunset is an enjoyable part of the liveaboard lifestyle, but I recommend no alcohol at all before or while you're cruising.

In addition to the safety concerns, BUI (boating under the influence) laws can be stricter (with higher fines and longer jail times) than DUI offenses. Just don't do it.

When it comes to following safety rules, I like to look at it this way. If you were working in a hospital and your job was to move several babies from one group of cribs to another group, how many babies would it be ok to drop? There should be zero mistakes when it comes to boating safety also.

## Cruising Can Be Dangerous

My uncle said that all of the land he ever wanted to own was enough to grow one African violet, and that's what he did. He had a flowerpot on his boat with one African violet. It always had beautiful blooms. I think his spirit describes a lot of liveaboards.

Unfortunately, he got caught in a storm off the coast of Florida. Pieces of his boat were found, but his body never was. That happened a long time ago, but the story still comes up in the family get-togethers from time to time. It's a constant reminder to me to respect the ocean and to always be aware that sailing can be dangerous.

## Security

I think of security in two situations:

1. **When the boat is in a marina.** When you're in a marina, there is not much risk to your personal safety. One scream and several nearby liveaboards with loaded guns would be there in a heartbeat. The real risk is that someone will steal equipment from your boat while you're not there. Boats are not as secure as a house. A large screwdriver and a bolt cutter will get you into most boats. Marinas that have adequate lighting and a gated entrance to the

dock area are a deterrent to would-be thieves. An alarm on the door to your cabin helps too.

2. **When you're cruising.** When you're sailing the high seas, you do have to worry about modern day pirates. In some parts of the world they are mainly interested in kidnapping the people on the boat for a ransom. In the Caribbean, drug dealers want to rob you and steal your boat. In either case, insurance will cover your boat. It's your personal safety that you are most concerned about.

You can be armed, but more than likely the professional pirates are better armed than you are. One recent case that was in the news described how a boat owner successfully fought off pirates with a shotgun. A shotgun can do a lot of damage to a boat at close range.

Of course, when you're carrying firearms onboard, make sure you have the proper permits. If you're going into international ports, be extra sure that you have all of the permits and approvals that you need. You can spend a lot of time in a foreign prison if you violate gun laws in some countries—Mexico comes to mind.

**Bottom line:** This chapter only scratches the surface of what you need to know about boating safety. I highly recommend that you take some boating classes, read other books, become familiar with Coast Guard and other boating safety websites, as well as spend time with an experienced captain and learn as much as you can about boating safety.

# Chapter 21:

## Government Regulations

*"Politicians and diapers must be changed often and for the same reason."*

~ Mark Twain

Boaters don't usually vote in the areas where they have parked their boat (and even if they did, there are not enough of them for politicians to pay any attention to them). On top of that, state, local, and federal governments seem to think boaters are wealthy and fair game for being taxed and regulated.

You can rant and rave about it, but then get over it. It's a fact of life. Fill out all of the forms, pay your taxes and fees, know and obey all of the laws, rules and regulations in your area, and get on with enjoying the liveaboard lifestyle.

## You Don't Have Any Rights or Expectation of Privacy as a Liveaboard

The biggest thing to be aware of is that, as a liveaboard, you do not have any right to privacy or freedom from unreasonable search and seizures like you did when you lived on land.

The Coast Guard (as well as other federal, state, and local authorities) is legally allowed to board and search your boat at any time (even in the middle of the night) and can do it at gunpoint. You have no legal right to resist, and if you do, you can find yourself in jail in a heartbeat.

If they find anything illegal (missing safety equipment, improper lights at night, missing or improper registration, your sewer valve in the wrong position, etc.), you could (and probably will) be fined and maybe even hauled off to jail if the infraction is serious enough.

If they find anything that makes them believe that a crime has been committed on the boat or that it has been used in the commission of a crime, they can immediately seize your boat and everything on it. They can do this even if they only suspect that a crime has been committed. If they find a single marijuana joint they can seize your boat.

In South Florida a lot of boaters jokingly describe the size of a boat as a "two-bailer" or a "three-bailer", etc. referring to how many bales of marijuana the boat could haul. I would be careful about using those terms in public places, like a bar or restaurant. Remember that if authorities, "suspect that a crime has been committed," they can seize your boat. If you like your boat, don't risk it.

Note that the federal law has been amended and now the law requires that *it is more likely than not that a crime was committed* before they can keep your boat, but many state and local laws still only require that the authorities suspect that a crime was committed.

When I say they can seize your boat, I don't mean that they will temporarily hold it: I mean they will keep it and use it or sell it, but, either way, it's their boat. You may think it's not fair, but it's the law. You can spend a lot of money on lawyers, but you won't win. Hopefully, you will have time to kiss your boat goodbye when they seize it but probably not.

Unless you have plenty of money to buy another boat (and don't mind spending some time in jail), make sure that nothing illegal happens on your boat. Even if you didn't personally do anything illegal and didn't know about it, you're the captain and should have known. It's your responsibility.

Sometimes with a minor violation there is some wiggle room, so it's important that you welcome the authorities on board, be nice, polite, and fully cooperate with their requests. It's a good idea to always be expecting the authorities to show up. Know where your safety gear, registration, and other papers are located and be able to put your hands on everything immediately.

Just as there are DUI (driving under the influence) laws, there are BUI (boating under the influence) laws. In some jurisdictions, the laws for BUI are even more stringent that DUI laws. A lot of boating accidents are caused by intoxicated boaters.

Some of these laws and things that the Coast Guard can do may not seem fair, but I'm glad they exist. They help keep boaters safe.

## International Ports

If you're cruising and going into ports in countries outside of the United States, there are a lot of other laws you'll need to comply with. And not following the laws of the jurisdiction of other countries could be more serious than violating US laws. For example, drug laws carry a much more serious punishment in many countries (even first-time offenses) than they do in the US.

Other international laws to be aware of are gun laws, pets may need to be quarantined, most fruits and vegetables (and even potted plants) may not be allowed, and everyone on board will need passports and may require proof of vaccinations. Everyone may need visas.

In other words, thoroughly check out all of the laws and regulations of any country you plan to enter and don't push the limits or try to get by with even minor transgressions. Even if other boaters tell you that certain ports are not very strict, don't risk it. They may not be strict most of the time, but that doesn't mean you won't get into trouble.

## Summary

The laws and rules I'm pointing out are not all bad. Most of these laws are necessary to keep the waterways safe and to prevent criminals from smuggling drugs and weapons into the country.

As a liveaboard, you will be subject to a lot more laws and regulations than you're used to, and most of them have serious consequences if you violate them. Most of these laws are for the safety and wellbeing of you and other boaters. Even if you don't agree with all of them or you don't think some of them are fair, you need to come to the realization that you're going to follow them to the letter or else not choose the liveaboard lifestyle.

**Bottom line:** Take safety and security seriously and follow the recommendations in this chapter to the letter. Don't try to cut corners or be lax when it comes to these matters.

If you tend to do things that violate laws that you think are not really important (such as driving 10 mph over the speed limit, smoking a joint from time to time, drinking too much on occasions, throwing trash out the window while you're driving or not paying close attention to paperwork and renewal dates) the liveaboard lifestyle may not be the right lifestyle for you.

# Chapter 22

# To Make It Happen You Have to Set a Date

*"Every man dies. Not every man really lives."*

~ William Wallace

If three birds were sitting on a fence, and one decided to fly away, how many would be left? If birds are anything like people, more than likely, there would still be three birds sitting on the fence. Just because one bird decided to fly away, doesn't mean that he actually did it. We decide to do things all the time but never get around to doing them.

Don't let your dream of living full time on a boat be just that—a dream. Take action.

## Three Things You Need to Do

1. Make a decision.

2. Set a date.

3. Make it happen.

You need to do a little bit of planning, but it shouldn't take forever. I know people who have spent two or three years planning and trying to decide if they should venture out and try living on a boat. There's no research you can do in two years that you can't do in two months.

### Make a Decision

Finish reading this book (refer back to certain chapters from time to time when you need to). If you didn't stop and check out the links to articles, websites, and videos as you were reading the book, go back and check out the links and watch the videos now. Do this and you will have a lot more information to help you make your decision.

When it comes to making your decision, there's one important thing to do, and that is to be sure to listen when you're discussing this with your spouse. Make sure it's something you both want to do.

I have had several people tell me that their plan was to do it for a year or two, but after they had gotten into the lifestyle, they didn't want to go back to a "normal" life. And I've seen it go the other way too.

Keep in mind that you can change your mind. You can sell your boat (maybe even at a profit if you've followed the techniques in the previous chapters about how to find and buy a boat at a bargain price).

My guess is that, even if you decide that the boating lifestyle is not what you want to do, you will probably not want to go back to your life just as it is now. You're ready for a change. Maybe you'll want to live in a different location such as a warmer climate or maybe you'll decide you want to try living in one place in the winter and another place in the summer. Whatever you do, make your decision, start living your new, exciting life and change your plans later if you choose to.

**Set a Date**

As long as you plan to live the boating life someday, it will never happen. The time will never be just perfect. The best way to make your dream a reality is to set a date.

Set a date that's realistic but ambitious. If you're leasing an apartment, when is your lease up? That could be a good date. After you set a date, mark it on your calendar, and tell your family and friends. Then it's no longer a dream; it's a matter of fact. Consider throwing a going away party for yourselves. This will make the fact that you really are going to move onto a boat on your announced date a reality.

**Make it Happen**

There are lots of ways you can go about getting ready to live on a boat. I know of one couple who bought their boat a year before they actually started living on it full time. They docked it at a nearby marina and lived on it off and on for the year. This allowed them to get used to the idea. They packed and repacked their boat and made some modifications to it. This gave them time to get rid of all of their stuff. They also put their house on the market and sold it during the year. The day they closed on the house, they moved onto their boat for good.

There are a lot of things that have to be done before you can make your dream of living life on a boat come true. Everything has to fall (or be pushed) into place to make your boating lifestyle a reality. There are so many things you have to do or make decisions about that it's hard to know where to start. It can seem overwhelming.

## The Easiest Way to Get Started Is to Make a Plan and Then Convert It Into a To-Do List

If you own a house, getting it sold or rented will probably be one of your biggest obstacles. Take steps to solve this problem first. Call a real estate agent and get your house on the market to sell or rent.

Don't sit idle and wait for the house to sell. Since you've already set a date when you're going to move onto your boat, get busy taking care of the other things that must be done.

A word about selling your house. I know people who have had their houses on the market for two or three years, and they still haven't sold them. A lot of people have an unrealistic expectation of what their house is worth. Don't fall into that trap. It's worth what it will sell for now. The main reason a house doesn't sell is that the owner has set an unrealistic price. Set your price at a fair market value (or maybe a little less) and your house will sell.

I've heard people say that they're going to wait for the housing market to rebound. If you really thought housing prices were going to go up 15% to 20% within the next year, wouldn't you be buying real estate like mad?

Put your house on the market, set a fair price and if it doesn't sell within a reasonable time, lower the price and keep doing this until it sells or until you decide to keep the house and rent it out. At that point, get it rented.

One other thing to be prepared for is that your house might sell within a few days. I was talking to a couple at a marina yesterday, and they said they had a contract on their house three days after they put it on the market. They had to get rid of everything and vacate the house in 30 days. Normally, getting a contract on your house is a good thing, but if you're not ready for it to sell, you might just have to get ready pretty quickly.

A few years ago, a friend had her place on the market for over a year and then finally sold it for less than she had turned down a month after it was listed. Your house is worth what it will sell for now—not what you think it's worth and not what it was worth a few years ago.

My parents sold their house (and a lot of the stuff inside it) at an auction. Maybe you're not that brave, but a good auction company will get a fair price for your house. I'm not recommending that you have an auction to sell your house, but if all else fails, it's an option.

While your house is on the market, get rid of all of your stuff that you don't need—which will be almost everything. How to get rid of your stuff was explained in chapter 16. It's easier than you think.

If you don't have a deadline, you will never get to the end of your to-do list.

## Not Everything Has to Be Done before You Move Aboard Your Boat

You're not like Lewis and Clark heading off into the wilderness for two years. You can do things while you're living on your boat.

Concentrate on taking care of the things that absolutely must be taken care of before you move onto your boat. Of course, one of those things is to buy a boat. That should be high on your list. If you need the equity in your house in order to buy it, you can still start looking at boats and doing your homework and deciding what kind of boat you want.

Remember, you have a move aboard date. If you didn't get your riding lawnmower sold, give it to someone. You'll be surprised how fast things happen when you really do have a firm departure date.

Of course, you always have the option of renting a storage unit for those items you're not ready to part with or those you would regret losing if living on a boat doesn't live up to your expectations.

Once you've made the decision to try living on a boat, don't waste time second-guessing yourself. Six months or a year down the road you can reevaluate the situation and, if living on a boat isn't making you happy, you can sell your boat and buy or rent a house or condo and live wherever you wish. You're not locked into your boating decision permanently.

By now you probably know that the boating lifestyle is for you. In your mind, you've already moved in. But as you start to think about the thousands of decisions you will have to make, you may begin to feel overwhelmed.

## Don't Over-analyze

There will always be unknowns and, as Yogi Berra said,

*"It's tough to make predictions, especially about the future."*

Now is your chance, while you're still young enough and healthy enough to enjoy the boating lifestyle, to make a decision with the main criteria being, "What lifestyle will I enjoy the most?"

The good part is that, by reading this book, you've found out that the lifestyle that may give you the most enjoyment won't cost you nearly as much as your current lifestyle. I think you've realized that scaling your expenses and obligations back and living a totally different lifestyle could bring you a lot more enjoyment and a lot less stress than you're experiencing now.

Take the facts, observations and inside information from this book and picture yourself living the boating lifestyle versus your present lifestyle and think about which way you would be happier. Of course, I think you've already done that.

## Things Don't Make You Happy. Experiences and Adventures Make You Happy

It's easier not to make a decision and just do what you've always done, but if you end up not changing your lifestyle, let it be because you considered all of the options and came to the conclusion that living your present lifestyle is what would make you the happiest. Don't let it be because you just never got around to making a decision.

My guess is that, since you've read this far into the book, you've already made your decision.

If you decide that living on a boat is the lifestyle for you, go for it. It could mean the start of the happiest years of your life. Take the plunge (maybe that's the wrong word—I don't want you to fall overboard).

I'll just sum things up by saying, "**To be happy you have to make your own decisions and grow your own daisies.**"

Mark Twain summarized the idea much better than I can when he wrote the following words:

*"Twenty years from now you will be more disappointed by the things you didn't do than by the ones you did do. So throw off the bowlines, sail away from the safe harbor. Catch the trade winds in your sails. Explore. Dream. Discover."*

~ Mark Twain

**Bottom line:** You made your decision before you got to this chapter. This chapter is to show you how to make it happen. As you get closer to your move aboard date, it will start to feel like crunch time. There will be a ton of things that will still need to be done and not much time to do them. Don't give in to changing your move aboard day. If you change it once, you'll change it again and again, and the process could drag out forever.

You've handled crunch time and deadlines all your life; you can handle one more. This one is important. Make it happen.

# Chapter 23:

---

# Summing It All Up

---

*"There are no foreign lands. It is the traveler only who is foreign."*

~ Robert Louis Stevenson

Since you've read this far into the book, my guess is that your mind is about made up. You're going to live on a boat. You probably still have a lot of questions, but you're ready to set your plan in action and make it happen.

As I said in the previous chapter, to make it happen you have to set a date. So start giving it some serious thought and set a date. Make it a realistic date, but also make it an ambitious one. You don't want it to be just a dream. It's really going to happen.

Keep in mind that when you make it happen, you will be living the dream of millions of people who have the dream but will never fulfill their dream. To them it will always only be a dream.

## Here Are Some Final Thoughts and Observations

- You will get to live with the same view of the water with sunrises and sunsets that many landlubbers are paying millions of dollars for.

- Don't spend too much on your first boat. Buy less boat than you can afford. You can add equipment or upgrade to a bigger boat later.

- When selecting your boat, choose comfort over performance unless you really plan to do a lot of cruising. After all, it will be your home.

- Start reading boating, sailing, and liveaboard books, watch videos, read discussion forums, cut back on your TV watching. You have a lot to learn before you become a liveaboard.

- Be a crew member on as many different boats as you can finagle your way onto.

- If you like to tinker and fix or modify things, a boat always has something that needs attention. If you don't like to fix things, a boat still always has things that need your attention.

- Living on a boat forces you to stay organized. Everything has a place, and everything has to stay in its place.

## It's Time to Make Your Decision

By now you have enough facts to make your decision about whether living on a boat is how you want to live your life. You could say that you want to get more information, but that's just a way of procrastinating. Of course, you don't know everything about being a liveaboard yet, but, as the professor said one time when I was sitting in on a Harvard marketing class, "Every decision you make for the rest of your life will be made with incomplete information."

My thoughts are that if you're not sure by now that you want to live the liveaboard lifestyle, it's probably not the lifestyle for you. Millions of people dream of being a liveaboard, but they never do it. It's not that they decide not to do it; most of them just never get around to making the decision either way.

Let's face the facts. It's not the right lifestyle for most people, but my guess is that since you've read this far, it highly likely that it is the right lifestyle for you.

Next, go to the *Other Resources* section and continue reading books, blogs, and discussion forums; watch videos and visit websites. With some effort, you can become one of the most knowledgeable liveaboards on the planet (well, at least you can become knowledgeable enough to get by).

Take the time to learn about sailing, diesel engines, weather, different kinds of boats and their advantages and disadvantages, navigation, boating safety, boating terminology, and the list of what you should learn goes on and on. I also recommend that you read some novels (and watch some YouTube videos) about boating adventures.

**Bottom line:** As of now, boating is in your blood. Your next step is to set a date and make it happen. The timing will never be perfect, so make it happen now and start enjoying your new lifestyle.

I think the whole liveaboard experience is summed up by the title of the classic Christmas movie with James Stewart, *It's a Wonderful Life.*

If you have questions for me, feel free to email me at Jminchey@gmail.com.

---

# Chapter 24

# Boating Terminology

---

*"A ship is safe in harbor, but that is not what a ship was built for."*

~ William H. Shedd

Boaters have their own words for a lot of things. You need to learn these to be accepted as a real liveaboard. For example, you can go to the store and buy a rope, but when you get it on the boat, it's no longer a piece of rope. It's a line.

If you are a beginning boater, you will discover quite a few nautical terms (and boating slang) that will not make any sense to you. Below is a list of some of the most common terms you are likely to come across.

These are not all of the boating terms that you will come across, but I think I have included the most common ones. I sometimes think boaters have so many special terms that it can seem like they have their own language.

You don't have to learn all of these immediately. Just refer to this section of the book when you come across a term that you don't understand.

## Here Are Some Boating Terms You Might Come Across

AFT – This is the direction toward the back end, or stern, of the boat.

Ballast – The material used to provide stability to a sailboat.

Beam – This refers to how wide a boat is.

Berth – This is another name for a bed.

Bilge - This is the lowest part of the boat. It's below the waterline. It's where the two sides meet at the keel. When water gets in the boat, this is where it collects and this is where you have to pump it from.

Bilge pump – The pump used to pump water out of the bottom of the boat. It's a good idea to carry a backup bilge pump. Bilge pumps fail and not having a working bilge pump could be a big problem in foul weather. Some cruisers carry two backup bilge pumps.

Bimini – A piece of canvas that you place over the cockpit to block out the sun.

Black water – This is the water in the tank from the toilet. Black water is another phrase meaning sewage.

Bow – This is a common term you will hear. It means the front part of the boat.

Bung – A stopper such as a truncated cylindrical or conical closure to stop up a hole in the side of a boat. It's like a cork for a really large bottle of wine.

BUI – Means Boating Under the Influence. It's the same as DUI, except the fines and penalties are usually higher. A lot of boating accidents are caused by people drinking too much alcohol and then trying to operate their boat. It's dangerous. Don't do it.

Courtesy lights – This refers to dim white or amber lights that are also referred to as mood lights. People use them sometimes for parties, etc.

Dinghy – This is a little boat that you drag along behind your big boat. It's used get you back and forth between your big boat and the shore. A dinghy may have a little motor or it may just have oars.

Dock lines – These are the ropes that tie the boat to the dock.

EPIRB – Emergency Position Indicating RadioBeacon. They cost from $200 to $1,500.

Galley – You probably know this term. It's the kitchen of a boat.

GMDSS – Global Maritime Distress & Safety System.

Gray water – This is the water from the shower and the kitchen sink.

Hanger locker – As the name implies, it's a small closet where you can hang a few clothes.

Head – There are two common meanings of this word. It actually means the toilet, but a lot of the time the bathroom is also referred to as the head.

Headsail – (Note: This is not a sail for the bathroom.) A headsail is any sail that is set forward of the foremost mast. The most common headsails are staysails, a term that includes jibs and the larger genoa.

Holding tank – Most boats will have three holding tanks. One will hold the fresh water, another for gray water and a third one for black water. The gray and black water tanks will be pumped out from time to time at the marina. It's illegal in most places to just dump either tank in the surrounding water.

Jib – It's the little sail out front. If you want to know more, it's a triangular staysail that sits ahead of the foremast. Small boats can be sailed using a jib alone. It is most commonly used to make a minor direct contribution to the propulsion. Generally, a jib's most crucial function is as an airfoil, increasing the performance and overall stability by reducing turbulence on the main sail's leeward side.

Knot – This is the boating term for speed. It's like mph, except not exactly equal. One knot is equal to 1.15 miles per hour.

Liveaboard – This word has two meanings. It means a boat that is used as a full-time home. It also means the person who lives full time on the boat. When you move onto your boat, you will be a liveaboard.

Main cabin – As the name implies, it's the main part of the boat that you live in. It is also sometimes called a salon. You can think of it as the same as the living room in a house.

Mooring – It's basically the same as being tied to an anchor, but you're tied to a ball that's tied to a heavy, sunken concrete block. You usually have to pay a setup fee and then a small monthly fee to use the system, but it's about half the cost of renting a dock at a marina. It's an alternative to living on the hook. A lot of the mooring fields are owned by cities or counties.

On the hard – This means the boat is sitting on something hard (like blocks or a cradle) instead of being in the water. This is done when the bottom is being painted or other work is being done to the bottom.

On the hook – The hook is the anchor, so it means that the boat is tied to the anchor instead of to a dock. Living on the hook is when a boat is out in the water and is tied to the anchor. You don't pay rent when you're living on the hook.

Pedestal – This is the control panel for a boat. It's a post in the cockpit that has the steering wheel and engine controls mounted on it. A pedestal is also the post at the dock where the power and water connections are located.

Port – This is the left side of the boat.

Portlight – This is another name for a window.

Pure sine wave inverter – An inverter is used to convert the 12-volt battery voltage into 110 volt AC to operate regular house appliances. You can get cheap inverters, called modified sine wave inverters, that are good for some appliances, but most electronics (TVs, radios, breathing machines, computers, etc.) require (or at least are less likely to be damaged by) an inverter that puts out a pure sine wave, which is what the waveform of ordinary shore power looks like. Bottom line: Get a pure sine wave inverter if you can afford it and maybe carry a cheap ($29) modified sine wave inverter as a backup.

Raw water – This is water that the boat is floating in that comes into the boat because you want it to. This is water that's used for cooling the engine, flushing the toilet, etc.

Running rigging – The lines that raise, lower, and adjust the sails on a sailboat. As mentioned at the start of this chapter, ropes are called lines when they're on the boat.

Slip – The space at a marina where you tie your boat up. It's where you live at a marina.

Standing rigging – These are the wire cables that support the mast and make sure that the mast (or masts) stand up and stay vertical on a sailboat.

Starboard – The right side of a boat.

Stern – The back of a boat.

Wet locker – A closet where you can hang wet clothes, such as rain gear or swimming suits.

**Bottom line:** These are by no means all of the words and phrases that you will come across, but read over these a few times and get familiar with them. Then, as you come across more boating phrases, just Google them, and soon you will be as knowledgeable as any old sea captain.

# Chapter 25:

---

# Other Resources

---

*"Someone asked me, if I were stranded on a desert island what book would I bring. . . How to Build a Boat."*

~ Steven Wright

Today there's an almost unlimited amount of information available about living on a boat, sailing, and boating topics in general. Thanks to the internet, a lot of this information is available free to you while you're sitting at home. Even most of the books you have to pay for are available in eBook format for $2.99 or so.

The links to the YouTube videos, books, forums, and websites I've listed below may not necessarily be the best, but they are some of my favorites. For sure, they don't cover everything you need to know, but they're a good start.

## YouTube Videos I Like

**Below are some links to YouTube videos showing the cruising liveaboard lifestyle:**

https://www.youtube.com/watch?v=CkaH_UUH0Ek

https://www.youtube.com/watch?v=sF9TNM9R-iw

https://www.youtube.com/watch?v=21e0fp48tqk

https://www.youtube.com/watch?v=6p9F4sSzMW0

## Here Are Some Links to YouTube Videos Showing Liveaboards Living at a Marina:

https://www.youtube.com/watch?v=g8Rbt1u2Ljs

https://www.youtube.com/watch?v=KKkNKEJ_Pfg

## YouTube Videos Showing How to Sail a Boat:

https://www.youtube.com/watch?v=yqwb4HIrORM

Here's a link to Part 1 of a series of videos showing a lot of details covering how to sail a boat. Watch the whole series and you will know a lot about sailing, but you will still need some hands-on experience.

https://www.youtube.com/watch?v=TttqFylquFs

## More Videos to Watch:

As you watch the videos I've referenced, you will notice that for every video you watch, YouTube will recommend other videos that you might like. Click on one of these videos and then "lather, rinse, and repeat" until you've spent an evening watching sailing, liveaboard, and boating videos in general. Do this instead of watching television and I think you will find this endeavor provides a much more enjoyable evening, and you'll learn a lot.

## Books I Like:

I recommend that you read several books about boating, sailing, and living on a boat by different authors.

One of the first ones you should own (other than this one, which you already own) is the first one on the list below. I think you'll like the others too.

- *The Essentials of Living Aboard a Boat*, by Mark Nicholas. Here is the link to it:
  http://www.amazon.com/dp/0939837668

- *Sail With Me: Two People, Two Boats, One Adventure*. Here's the link to it: http://www.amazon.com/dp/0692321799

- *Navigation Rules: International – Inland*. Here's the link to it: http://www.amazon.com/dp/0939837498

- *Dutton's Nautical Navigation*, 15th Edition. Here's a link to it: http://www.amazon.com/gp/product/155750248X

- *This Old Boat, Second Edition: Completely Revised and Expanded*. Here's a link to it:

  http://www.amazon.com/dp/0071477942

In addition to reading how-to books, I recommend that you read some novels about sailing and living on a boat. I've found that I have learned a lot about sailing, about dealing with storms, and about living on a boat in general while reading entertaining novels.

## Forums I Like:

I also recommend that you read a lot of posts on several different forums. One of the things I like about forums is that many of them have been around for a very long time and during that time almost every question you can imagine has been answered. This means that you don't have to ask your question. You can just use the search feature and search the archives of the forum and find the answer to your question. That's what I usually do.

## Here Some Forums That I Recommend:

SailNet.com

CruisersForum.com

Life-Aboard.com

## Websites I Like:

**Below are links to two websites that have a lot of useful safety information:**

http://www.usps.org/index.html

http://powerboat.about.com/od/safetyandeducation/tp/Boating-Best-Practices.htm

**Here are three websites that have good general liveaboard information:**

http://www.LivingAboard.net

http://www.SleepingWithOars.com

http://GoneWithTheWynns.com

**Bottom line:** If you're considering becoming a liveaboard, realize that there is a lot to learn in order to safely and economically enjoy the liveaboard lifestyle. Check out the links in this chapter and you will be well on your way to being an informed and experienced liveaboard.

# About the Author

*"I can resist everything except temptation."*
~ Oscar Wilde

Jerry Minchey is an electrical engineer, author, and business owner. He has a Bachelor's degree in Electrical Engineering, an MBA from USC, and an OPM degree from Harvard Business School.

He worked for NASA and worked for many years as a computer design engineer. He has five patents and a private pilot's license with an instrument rating. He also enjoys playing old-time mountain fiddle music.

As an engineer and a business manager, he looks at problems from a logical standpoint as well as an economical and financial standpoint. He has written 11 books following this format of analysis and presentation.

####

Printed in Great Britain
by Amazon